ANGLISTICA

VOL. XI

ANGLISTICA

EDITORS

TORSTEN DAHL
AARHUS

KEMP MALONE
BALTIMORE

GEOFFREY TILLOTSON
LONDON

VOL. XI

ROSENKILDE AND BAGGER
COPENHAGEN 1958

PATER ON STYLE

An examination of the essay on "Style" and the textual
history of "Marius the Epicurean"

BY

EDMUND CHANDLER

ROSENKILDE AND BAGGER
COPENHAGEN 1958

IN MEM.

H. C. C.

1884—1950

Copyright 1958 by Rosenkilde and Bagger. Printed in Denmark by Bogtrykkeriet Antikva, Copenhagen.

PREFACE

A few words are probably necessary to explain the microscopic nature of the following study.

It originated as a thesis accepted by the University of London for the degree of Master of Arts. I have added comparatively little for this version, for an overwhelming reason.

I have naturally looked at everything that I could lay my hands on about Pater — the total volume is not large. And I feel bound to say that most of what goes for biography and criticism of Pater is, in my opinion, frankly unsatisfactory. Because there is no single volume devoted to Pater that I found acceptable, I decided when writing the study to avoid as far as possible all references to other works: the omission of footnotes and references is therefore deliberate.

It is still difficult to write about Pater dispassionately, principally, I believe, because the assumptions of the Aesthetic Movement continue to dominate most critical writing today. For my own part, I have tried to deal in facts only and to be as objective as possible in judgments: but since no work can be totally free from bias, I ought in honesty to mention that my deepest feelings towards Pater's work are antipathetic rather than otherwise.

When I was invited to prepare this for publication, I thought I might try to straighten out some of the current biographical and critical misconceptions. But I have found that a much greater task than I imagined, and beyond my present capacity. So I finally thought it best to include here only what could stand on its own feet — to stick rigidly to my frame of reference. I hope, however, that what has come to light even in this small field is enough to show how much Pater is worth further study, and that at least it will be of help to the biographer and critic that Pater urgently needs.

I should like, in conclusion, to thank Professor Geoffrey Tillotson for the original suggestion of this study and for his help in many tangible and intangible ways; and the Governors of Birkbeck College for their great generosity in making publication possible.

CONTENTS

INTRODUCTION

In 1880 Pater resigned his tutorship at Brasenose College in order to devote his time exclusively to writing. During the next four years he was occupied almost solely with his only completed 'novel', *Marius the Epicurean*, for over this period nothing appeared from his pen except a memorial essay, "Dante Gabriel Rossetti", in 1883. *Marius the Epicurean* was eventually published in February, 1885. Its success was immediate, enthusiastic notices appearing in such papers as the *Saturday Review* and the *Pall Mall Gazette*. And perhaps significantly with the completion of his longest and most ambitious work, Pater then moved to London for the first time in his adult life, and took a house in Earls Terrace, Kensington, where he began to follow a much wider social life than hitherto.

The next three years were prolific. A second edition of *Marius* was called for in 1885, and was issued in November. For this edition the type was reset and a different format was used, no doubt owing to the number of corrections and emendations Pater made to the text of the first edition, and to the suppression of one substantial passage. Within this same year, according to the bibliography prefixed to the posthumous volume *Miscellaneous Studies*, Pater wrote the essay "A Prince of Court Painters"; and the three other essays that went to make up the volume *Imaginary Portraits* were written in the following year, 1886. "Sir Thomas Browne" and "Feuillet's 'La Morte'", which were later to appear in *Appreciations*, also belong to the year 1886. *Gaston de Latour*, the companion piece of *Marius*, appears to have been well in hand by the early half of 1888, starting its serial publication in *Macmillan's Magazine* in June.

In August, 1888, there appeared in the *Pall Mall Gazette* a review by Pater of a volume of the *Life and Letters of Gustave Flaubert*. This review was expanded and appeared again, in December of the same year in the *Fortnightly Review*, as an essay now entitled "Style", and was reprinted in its entirety as the first essay in the volume *Appreciations*, published in 1889. "Style" has long attracted attention; and from its urgency and, for Pater, unusual directness of statement, it has been taken, by A. C. Benson and Edward Thomas particularly, as in the nature of a personal testament.

Gaston de Latour suddenly ceased its serial publication in October, 1888, and was never again taken up by Pater. To the following year, 1889, the bibliography mentioned ascribes only two minor essays — "Hippolytus Veiled" and "Giordano Bruno" — and to the year 1890 the slight "Art Notes in Northern Italy" and the lecture "Prosper Merimee". Nothing appears to have been written in 1891; but in 1892 appeared a third and 'Revised' edition of *Marius the Epicurean*, containing over six thousand textual variations from the previous editions.

Pater frequently revised his published works. The textual alterations to the "Conclusion" to *Studies in the History of the Renaissance* (itself later changed to *The Renaissance: Studies in Art and Poetry)* are well known. In addition to textual variations, essays were occasionally suppressed from and added to existing volumes. None of these alterations, though, appears comparable to the total re-writing that *Marius* was subjected to. And the scale of the alterations, incidentally, suggests an intention that this was to be regarded as his major work.

Since the overwhelming majority of the variations in the text of *Marius* concern 'style' in that they do not materially affect the sense as it stands in the first and second editions, it seems clear that the revision owed its inspiration to the intervening essay on "Style", and that Pater considered the matter so important that he abandoned *Gaston de Latour* and devoted the greater part of the three years 1889—91 to it. The remaining two years of his life were as prolific as the years 1885—1888. The purpose, therefore, is to attempt to show the manner and extent that Pater applied the principles of the essay on "Style" when revising *Marius the Epicurean*.

To this end, I have given first a precis of "Style", considered necessary because, though not the most difficult of Pater's prose, there will no doubt always be room for a certain degree of interpretation on the part of the reader; this section therefore represents what I have myself understood by the essay. The principles thus established are then set out and examined in the next section in what is hoped is a more systematic, or at least more convenient, manner.

The fourth section is concerned with presenting the textual history of *Marius the Epicurean*. The length of the work and the extent of the changes make it superfluous to do it exhaustively, and the stylistic changes have therefore been classified into a number of empirical categories that suggested themselves in the course of collation. At the end of this section the small but important number of changes affecting meaning are examined, though they belong of course to a larger context.

The final section is given over to general conclusions and various leading ideas that emerge.

CHAPTER I

THE ESSAY ON "STYLE"

Pater begins the essay on "Style" by asserting it was inevitable in the natural order of things that a distinction should come to be made between poetry and prose, but that those who have insisted most on the distinction may have tended to circumscribe the functions of prose a little too closely. Any attempt to define the limits of an art from theory is always likely to be stultified by practice, and since prose has proved itself to be a medium of many colours, capable of the most diverse effects and purposes, it would be absurd to insist on *a priori* grounds that its nature limits it to, for instance, mainly practical interests. For many of the qualities a literary critic seeks for are to be found in poetry and prose alike, and it is therefore the duty of criticism to estimate the various excellencies of prose, as it exists, just as much as those of poetry.

Dryden was one who pleaded against the intrusion into prose of qualities first isolated in poetry, insisting that the cardinal virtue of prose must be the quality of mere 'correctness'. Wordsworth, on the other hand, and with a larger view, discounted the distinction between prose and poetry as one of form only, and claimed that the essential classification was rather between 'imaginative' and 'unimaginative' writing — De Quincey's "the literature of power and the literature of knowledge" — irrespective of form. In the "literature of knowledge" the author is concerned with the presentation of fact: in the "literature of power", with his own personal *sense* of fact.

Using this as a point of departure, Pater states he will indicate certain conditions of literature, criteria that apply both to the literature of knowledge and, especially, to the literature of power, regardless of form, and which may hold in their generality the virtues and the excellencies that will help in both the discrimination and the preservation of good prose.

The difference in these two kinds of writing, especially when they occur in the same work, cannot be demonstrated exactly — the point, that is, where an author turns from exposition and argument, to pleading.

In the literature of fact, the primary virtue is the author's ability to transcribe bare facts into words; but even so, there are many seemingly factual writings where the author has superimposed his personal sense of fact, if only in the selection and order of the particular facts he presents. And in proportion as the author's aim comes to be rather the presentation of his own sense of fact, so his work becomes 'fine' art; the intention of Pater's essay being to prove that the *truth* of the presentation of that personal sense of fact determines its quality as a work of art. Beauty can then be described as only *fineness* of truth, the exactness of the transcription into words of the vision within.

It is natural for any author to incline fact to his personal sense of its fitness and beauty. And in this action he is not alone: everything that men produce tends to have imposed, to the extent its function will bear, the producer's sense of beauty and fitness, and so aspires to 'fine' as opposed to 'serviceable' art. Literature, like the other arts that masquerade as 'facts' about human beings, or 'facts' as they affect human beings, can only represent those facts associated with a specific personality, in his individual ways and preferences.

The writing of imaginative literature can, therefore, be described as the transcription of fact as expressed by and concerning human beings in their infinite variety. Its quality as literary art will depend upon the truth of the expression of such 'soul-fact', whether the form be poetry or prose. In this connection, Pater claims, it may well be that imaginative prose is specially fitted as a medium for literary art in the modern world, for two reasons. Firstly, the chaotic complexity of its interests, and its conflicting principles and philosophies, produce a state of mind little disposed to the restraint of verse. Secondly, our curiosity about the natural world, and our concern with facts because they are facts, rather than with speculation, inevitably turns to what in the long run has come to be the less ambitious form of literature. And if it is true that imaginative prose is fitting to the modern temper, it will reflect that temper with all the variety and virtues of humanity itself.

The literary artist, Pater goes on to say, will necessarily be a scholar, and will presuppose always that the reader will go scrupulously and exactly over his work. A certain scholarship in words is necessary to the writer because his material is not his own creation. Language has a multitude of subtle and recondite laws and usages, and knowledge of them is the writer's necessary scholarship. Rather than being a hindrance, these laws and usages, if nicely observed, suffuse an impression of care and sensibility throughout his work. Harvesting from each word and phrase the maximum of its expression, he will, if he be fully sensitive to his vocabulary, have as his greatest care the excision of everything that could detract from his purpose. He must therefore know the affinities, avoidances and usages that have grown into the language in the course of literary history, all of which impose an abundance of demands on his vocabulary, and proscribe even the striking phrase if it be gipsy. His appeal, in this matter, must be to the taste and conscience of the scholar, and the care that he shows in the minutest detail, especially in such rejections and observances, will be a pledge to the sensible reader that he is dealing honestly and scrupulously, and a challenge to be treated precisely as carefully.

By such activity, by the discriminating and careful choice of his words, a literary artist builds a vocabulary that is true to himself and of which he can be truly master. Such discrimination, however, is not to be confused with pedantry, for knowledge of the laws of language implies also knowledge of the *value* of such laws; and hence the liberties he is able to take come to be indirect evidence of his good taste. The value of a deliberate vocabulary is perhaps best seen against the fashion among translators to aim for idiom and construction, whereas the truest reflection of a careful writer, Pater says, will lie in the most literal translation of his nouns and verbs, the skeleton and the elements of his work.

Since his choice of words reflects an author's personality, he must be for ever sifting his vocabulary for exacter words to express his interior vision. He should, for instance, be well aware of those words he would reject in any dictionary other than Dr Johnson's. And such authors, claims Pater, are the guardians of language in adapting it to the peculiar needs of their age and time — as, for instance, Wordsworth did, at the end of the eighteenth century. Recently the language had been taking over the phraseology of pictorial art, German metaphysics, and mystical theology; and it is predicted by Pater that in the near future a good deal of the vocabulary of natural science would be assimilated into the accepted language. The literary artist would therefore need to be aware of science, and to seek in it what it has to offer in the way of new modes and words. And as the greatest stimulus to good style is to have a rich and complex matter to grapple with, new concepts and words gained in this way will be of the utmost value and encouragement. Similarly, the writer can use his knowledge of the history of the language to restore finer meanings to those words that our 'business' has hackneyed and blunted: — words like 'ascertain', 'communicate', and 'discover'. And putting no value on the accidental origins of words as such, he will in his work mingle Latin and

Saxon words readily, the former with their directness and raciness, the latter with their euphony and "second intention", for no choice of words can at this stage help but be eclectic.

The literary artist, in observing these conditions, will also necessarily leave something to the reader's intelligence, and will shy from condescension and false simplicity. Active minds are stimulated by the challenge of a continuous effort, and value the pleasure that comes from eventual mastery of the author's meaning. And since there is beauty in restraint and economy in words, such a reader will take satisfaction in the frugal exactness of an author's language, in the manipulation that draws the utmost relief from each word and sentence, and the opportunity offered at every stage of the reading for the delightful sense of difficulty overcome.

Though there will be many kinds of readers, reading for many different purposes, the careful, discriminating reader will perhaps always regard literature as a sort of refuge, a relief from the somewhat vulgar world. The complete mastery and appreciation of a work performs for them something of the function of a religious retreat. The literary artist, writing with such readers as these principally in mind, will endeavour to maintain that literary ideal whereby every element of his work undergoes trial, especially eschewing any ornament or decoration not intrinsically necessary. In fact, his omissions may be the most significant mark of an author, for he will know how difficult it is to control figure and metaphor so that they do not distract attention and divert the imagination.

The scholarly attentiveness that has been mentioned is, of course, particularly alive to such waywardnesses, but the literary artist will allow for this in his knowledge that the "one beauty" of all literary style is essentially independent of removable ornament, and indeed exists in its fullest brilliance in works (such as *Madame Bovary* and *Le Rouge et le Noir)* with scarcely a suggestion of visible beauty. Aware, then, of the magnetic attraction of ornament to the negligent reader, and so of its destructiveness to his purpose, he will not depart from his ideal of exact expression other than for a considerable gain. All art, in this sense, can be said to be the "removal of surplusage", the filing of a matter down to its exactest expression. And what has been said of figure and metaphor applies also to the more subtle motions of language, the mixed metaphor that has become accepted speech, and the unwarranted extensions that daily afflict language.

Yet all these conditions, arising out of the nature of language and its behaviour, are subordinate to a more intrinsic quality of good style — the necessity, namely, of an intellectual, almost architectonic, conception of the work as a whole, implicit at every point — what Pater describes as the necessity of *mind* in style.

All the laws of good writing aim at an identity, almost, of the word with its object, so that the word, or sentence, or song, *seems to become what it says*. But this can only be achieved if the initial apprehension or intention is fully realised, and so in any work of art a strict logic of purpose in its unfolding is paramount — 'logic' being an appropriate metaphor here, since literature is of all arts the nearest to the abstract intelligence. When such a purpose is seen clearly, it will show through in every line of the work, in the choice of a particular word even, and the arriving there will be the more certain and masterful. And such logical coherence may demand, for instance, much variation in the building of sentences, and in the manner and pace of each part of the entire work. It may require the alternation of a brisk, sharp sentence with a long and intricate one; and if the work is to be richly expressive, the sentence born of foresight and certainty must share place with the sentence that shows growth and development in its elaboration, with many adjustments and irregularities which contribute to the whole. Perhaps all weakness of style, as Flaubert suggested, can be traced to uncertainty, to lack of a leading purpose or design, which results in accretion rather than composition. But if the literary artist holds to his purpose, to his particular view of the world, then his conclusion will write itself into his words, so that the end comes to him freshly and almost in surprise. The fact that some works appear the greater on second reading shows a deeper appreciation of this quality on the part of the reader. And although there have been writers able to achieve this effect unconsciously or by intuition, yet the reader's pleasure is often greatest where he can recognise the creative intelligence, and can critically trace it out in the parts of the work, for this constructive faculty is one of the forms of the imagination.

And there is also the quality of *soul* in style. Mind in style — the the intellectual quality — we cannot but appreciate when we see it, but the quality of soul has no such inevitable appeal. By it, is meant that faculty, most easily illustrated in religious writings but not necessarily pietistic, of instantaneous appeal to the sympathy of the reader because the words, by a strange alchemy, establish immediate and deep contact, as with some intimate revelation. Writers with the quality of 'soul' appear to absorb language and imbue it with their own peculiar spirit, so that the result seems to us like a fantastic inspiration. Perhaps their ability consists in choosing words that contribute to the unity of *atmosphere* they attain — as opposed to the unity of *design* in more conscious writers:

and where the quality of mind secures form, being definite, the quality of soul secures what Pater calls "colour" or "perfume", being indefinite.

Pater then digress into a discussion of Flaubert and the monumental labours that have earned him the title of the 'martyr' of style. Pater quotes a French critic describing Flaubert's principle of 'le mot juste', which, he believed, was the means to the quality in literary art (that is, 'truth') that lies beyond incidental and ornamental beauty. Flaubert's obsession with the thought that there exists the precise word or phrase for everything to be expressed shows, Pater suggests, the influence of a philosophical idea — that exact correlations between the world of ideas and the world of words can be found. Pater would have it, however, that the process is not so much of an existent idea in search of expression, as of the clarification of the thought itself — that is, that in a moment of difficulty it is not the correct word that is lacking, but confusion in the very idea itself: but he recognises Flaubert's method was intended to produce precisely the result that he has already commended. Yet whether the 'search' be long or short, easy or difficult, is ultimately irrelevant: the criterion in literary art is solely the *success* or otherwise of the result. And with Flaubert it is suggested that his labours were really directed not so much towards the perfection of style as against the facile and the otiose in art, which was his life-long aversion.

The discovery of the right expression, Pater claims, comes by a process that is not capable of strict analysis; and in that it is the result of an intuition, it calls for a similar act of intuition on the part of the reader for its recognition.

In all forms of literature then, the one indispensable beauty lies in the precision of the correspondence between thought and word — that is, by Pater's definition, truth. Such truth can be in relation to bare fact, as in scientific writing, or in the relation to insight and idea, as in imaginative writing; but in the latter, all other beauty associated with literature is in the service of this first ideal, thus justifying both the crisp, short sentence and the long intricate one, baldness in writing and elaborate ornament; and revisions and re-touchings are of value in this sense only in so far as they help to bring out the original intention and perception. 'The style is the man' then becomes true in that such an ideal of style must reveal, indirectly, the literary artist's peculiar sense of fact, and through that his personality in its complexity. But this is not to make style subservient to individuality, and thence to be equivalent to mannerism. For mannerism implies the false and insincere, which cannot enter into the scheme that has been suggested. What finally determines, and is critically appreciated, is the *matter*, and the literary artist is related only to that. Thus defined, as it is here, as essentially a *process*, style can only be in itself impersonal. And literature, in thus aiming at identity of form with matter, of subject with expression, is aspiring to the condition of music, which is also the condition of all good art.

The greatness of a work of art is another question; if the previous conditions have been observed, its greatness depends on such criteria as its dignity of matter, its general humanity, and whether it be devoted to the enlargement of human happiness.

CHAPTER II

PRINCIPLES OF THE ESSAY ON "STYLE"

Pater in this essay sees the prime condition of good writing to be
truth. In scientific writing, or any writing concerned only with imparting
facts, the truth to reality of the facts stated is obviously the thing of
value. The writer's task there is to find exact expression in words for a
particular series of facts, and if the words precisely represent things that
are true then the work will have value.

But so little writing, at least that the ordinary reader is concerned
with, comes within this category and calls for this sole criterion, that the
point is simple enough to be suspect. It appears, however, that it is made
for its use as a generalisation, so that it can be used subsequently as an
analogy to the case of literary art.

Pater uses the word 'art' to include all works where the author's personal 'sense of fact', his insight into any particular subject, is what is
primarily being communicated. In prose, literary art begins when the
author is presenting a subject *as seen by him*, and it is fine art according
to the degree of perception attained. The above criterion can then be
applied, by analogy, as the truth of the words to the perception within
the writer's mind. This truth, this fusion of word and insight, is for
Pater the "one beauty of all prose style": "all beauty is in the long run
only *fineness* of truth, or what we call expression, the finer accommodation
of speech to the vision within". Thus is the word 'beauty' introduced,
and identified as an aspect of his meaning of 'truth'.

Pater of course hereby pushes the problem of style further back than
words and makes it one of perception: "The first condition ... must be,
of course, to know yourself, to have ascertained your own sense exactly".
The problem for the author is to know precisely what he wishes to say,
to realise fully his own perception. And if this perfect realisation is
achieved and expressed, then it is inevitably a revelation of the author's
own personality, a portion of his own mind, and in such a sense 'the
style is the man'.

By presenting the matter in this way Pater is, he claims, meaning something quite other than Flaubert's dictum of 'le mot juste'. Pater points out the philosophical difficulty of Flaubert's principle, that it assumes "some pre-existent adaptation, between a relative, somewhere in the world of thought, and a correlative, somewhere in the world of language ...". But this aspect apart, the very concept of a 'search' for words is at variance with Pater's thought, and he goes out of his way to deprecate the idea. For what Flaubert imagines as an objective search, Pater conceives as a subjective scrutiny: that is, that you cannot begin to search for the word until you know precisely what you wish to say, and for which there is only one possible expression when you have determined it. But the story of Flaubert's labours for 'le mot juste' has captured imagination so effectively that Pater has to comment sharply we "may think that his almost endless hesitation had much to do with diseased nerves". Whether for any artist the transition from perception to expression comes easily or not is a personal matter, Pater feels, and of no artistic relevance. And Flaubert's labours, he claims, should be regarded rather as part of his lifelong war against the facile in art, which is related to but apart from literary style.

All imaginative writing that achieves perfect expression of the author's intent, and thence expression of his own being, Pater divides into two categories. The first, mentioned almost in order to be dismissed, is characterised as displaying the quality of 'soul' in style, because its appeal is not to the intellect but rather to some vagrant sympathy in the reader with which, by an obscure attraction, it makes immediate contact. Pater refers, by way of illustration, to such writers as Sir Thomas Browne, Jeremy Taylor, and the makers of the Authorised Version, whose work, read as literature, leaves a deep impression on the reader without his ever being quite able to define why, for certainly the conscious, intellectual part of it is negligible. When writing is capable of such effect we often describe it as having 'charm', the word itself a concession to the non-rational. The fact that such writing arrests at once or never at all, tends to confirm Pater's dismissal of it as beyond analysis. Pater is sensible of the quality, for the essay on 'Sir Thomas Browne', written in 1886, is a long attempt to grapple with it, succeeding only in resolving that it is an almost intimate revelation of personality, with the delicate appeal of a personal confession. Pater deals with this category of writing briefly, and the tone of his comments ("There are some to whom nothing has any real interest, or real meaning, except as operative in a given person; and it is they who best appreciate the quality of soul in literary art.") suggests a certain derogation.

It is the second category, that displays the quality of 'mind' in style, with which Pater is chiefly concerned. When the author has achieved his own personal sense of fact, when he has acquired "some strong and leading sense of the world" to inform his work, there will appear in it an overriding, architectonic conception of the work as a whole, for "in literary art as in all other art, structure is all-important". This quality is a logical consequence of Pater's previous condition of good writing or style, that the author must first know fully his own mind: "All depends on the original unity, the vital wholeness and identity, of the initiatory apprehension or view". Literary art, "being of all the arts most closely cognate to the abstract intelligence", will demand some form of progression, some development of its own logic, in the matter to be expressed. If there is this quality — what, for convenience, might be termed 'purpose' — it will suffuse itself throughout the work, dictating the dimensions of each part, adjusting the rhythm of the sentences, deciding the employment of particular words. Though never explicit, the *direction* that such a purpose gives to the whole work, the steady tone of authority behind the words, is what of course conveys that sense of mastery and certainty we associate with good literary style. It can be the bedrock upon which the structure is based, the fixed point of reference behind all that is said, or control thought and expression as a conductor an orchestra. And though it is only perceived in fragments, and not experienced entirely until the completion, it is the conscious sense of it, its deliberate reception into the mind, that forms one of the principal pleasures of reading. The reader traces it out, unravels the intricacies, an antenna of his mind reaching behind every sentence and paragraph for what it contributes to this sense, until eventually a whole new experience has been absorbed and he has acquired what (for him) is a new vision.

What here, in substance, has been said of literary art, is a matter of principle, Pater claims, that applies to all art. With the particular case of prose, Pater first considers the medium as such, and then draws a number of conclusions dependent on it, which should apply to all good writing. This is as far as Pater goes in considering the mechanics of literary style.

The artist in words is working with a material that "is no more a creation of his own than the sculptor's marble". The subtlety of language is almost infinite: in Pater's phrase, "Product of a myriad various minds and contending tongues, compact of obscure and minute associations", our knowledge of it, owing to its universality, can never be more than relative. The writer must obviously make it his perennial study, must be learned in its "abundant and often recondite laws", and this will form his "necessary scholarship". Just as no pianist is without a knowledge of the mechanism of the piano, his consciousness of the hammers helping him to control the tone of his playing, so the writer will need to know the mechanism or rules of language, in order more effectively to dispose his words. And observance of them will be noticed by the careful reader, who, seeing propriety and discrimination at work, will give the more willingly of his attention: "the attention of the writer, in every minutest detail, being a pledge that it is worth the reader's while to be attentive too". Knowledge of the laws of language, Pater adds, means also a knowledge of the value of such laws; unlike the pedant, who obeys the letter but not the spirit, he will show "his intelligence of the values of language in his freedom with it", as his own good taste permits.

In concrete terms, this means that the author must be for ever reviewing and recruiting his vocabulary. And for such work, Pater recommends the hard way: the writer, he says, must be "conscious of the words he would select in systematic reading of a dictionary, and still more of the words he would reject were the dictionary other than Johnson's". The writer is enjoined to make his selection of words "with his peculiar sense of the world ever in view", and to acquire those "faithful to the colouring of his own spirit". In his search, it is his business to remember that the language is always turning into common currency what once had been specialised vocabulary. Pater instances the phraseology of German metaphysics — presumably words like 'transcend', 'ideal', and 'phenomenon' — which came into general use in the latter half of the nineteenth century, and predicts (what time has justified) that the vocabulary of natural science would increasingly gain currency in the future. The writer, in turning such resources to his advantage, will necessarily need to be aware of subjects fruitful of new words and concepts. And parallel with the incorporation of new words, he can refurbish old ones which have become distorted through their use in business jargon — words like 'reference', 'ascertain', and 'communicate'. Pater also recommends a happy mingling of, rather than discrimination between, Latin words and Saxon: Saxon words being always direct and concrete, with a precise reference, and emotive aura, whereas Latin borrowings are usually abstract words, carrying resonance and implication: for "In this late day certainly, no critical process can be conducted reasonably without eclecticism".

Two faults of taste Pater then enumerates as especially dangerous for the writer. The first is the error of writing down: assuming always that his readers are his equals, and are willing to make an effort to understand his work, the author will "leave something to the willing intelligence of the reader". By his good taste in this matter, of course, a writer effectively chooses his audience. He will not retain sympathy if he offers "uncomplimentary assistance to the reader's wit", for the appreciation of a work of literature is a dialectic, and the reader must be given his part. A careful reader, says Pater, obtains pleasure from the exercise of his own mind on a work if he is promised, by the care and discrimination of the writing, a more thorough and complete mastery of the author's intention. There is for him, in that case, "the delightful sense of difficulty overcome", to add to his pleasure.

And the second error is the use of any kind of ornament. If the "one beauty of all good prose style" is the exact correspondence of the words with the author's perception, then any decoration is irrelevant and, even worse, destructive to the purpose. Anything not immediately related to his purpose, any addition for the mere sake of ornament, any parallel or allusion even, will act as a diversion for the vagrant mind and will call up its own peculiar train of associations, beyond the control of the author, and succeeding in nothing so much as detracting from his purpose. And the possibility of interference can arise not only from deliberate ornament, but from an incongruous word even, containing some reference or metaphor not related, and liable therefore to become obtrusive and acquire a life of its own. This danger, consequently, means that the author must always be pruning, and eliminating everything unrelated and inessential: "in truth all art does but consist in the removal of surplusage".

In the achievement of good style, then, the literary artist must first have 'vision', must know exactly his own personal sense of the world. In order to express it adequately in words, he must be familiar with the meaning of language, its behaviour and limitations, and must build his own original, necessarily eclectic vocabulary. And in the process his good taste must warn him of the dangers of condescension and ornament.

CHAPTER III

THE TEXTUAL HISTORY OF "MARIUS THE EPICUREAN"

Pater started to revise the text of *Marius the Epicurean* immediately it was published, and the number of alterations he made to the text for the second edition, issued only ten months after the first, may well have been one of the reasons why the type was re-set and, curiously, a different binding was used. (The second edition of *Marius* is remarkable for being the only book of Pater's published by Messrs Macmillans in his own lifetime that is not in the standard dark blue binding). The variations in the text are almost entirely in word order and punctuation; but there is also one passage in the first edition that was completely suppressed in the second and all other editions, and this passage, which will be given later, is so extraordinary for its sheer sadism that it seems to me unique in Pater and perhaps in English writing. It is tempting to suppose that the changes in type and binding were an attempt to disguise this suppression.

Apart from this passage, however, the variations in the text between the first and second editions are so few (numbering little more than a hundred) and so insignificant in comparison with the changes Pater made for the third edition, that I have largely disregarded them; and because the reasons he appears to have had for making the changes for the second edition are so much more fully and interestingly at work in the alterations for the third edition, I can see no reason for giving them special consideration in themselves. In the description of the textual history of *Marius* that follows, therefore, I have made use of the text of the first and third editions almost exclusively, and the text of the second edition is given only when it varies significantly from either.

The most striking fact about the alterations Pater made for the third edition is that they rarely affect the original sentence and paragraph structure. Pater's method was undoubtedly to revise the earlier editions sentence by sentence, and the great majority of the alterations are made within the context of the original sentence in meaning and shape. Words and phrases are added, omitted, and changed, and the punctuation is varied; but the sentences almost invariably remain similar in pattern and meaning to the version in the first and second editions. The number of new sentences created, mostly by the breaking of a sentence as it appears in the first edition, is very small, and the number of new paragraphs similarly created even smaller.

There are four chapters in particular, Chapters 8, 14, 16, and 22, where substantial revision of the sense has been undertaken, and where alterations have been made for reasons of meaning rather than style. These will be given in detail, but it is important to emphasise that they are a very small minority of the total number of alterations. It is also worth mentioning here that there are two extensive passages — the story of Cupid and Psyche, and the Platonic dialogue in Chapter 24 — where Pater leaves the text as printed in the first edition virtually intact.

Pater, then, has taken each sentence and attempted to give it a cleaner and clearer shape, a sharper outline, and a more precise impression, altering the sentence only in so far as the original thought could be better and more neatly expressed. The great majority of the textual alterations therefore consist of additions and omissions of, and changes in, words and phrases, changes in the word order, and variations (principally omissions) of punctuation. For illustration, it is felt it may be useful to give immediately an example of these changes in the text between the first and the third editions, and the following can be regarded as generally typical. The passages that are peculiar to each edition are italicised.

First edition

Certainly, there have been occasions when I have felt that if others cared for me as I *did* for them, it would be, not so much a *solace of loss,* as an equivalent for *it — a certain real thing in itself —* a touching of that absolute ground *among* all the changes of phenomena, such as our philosophers *of late have professed* themselves quite unable to *find.* In the mere clinging of human creatures to each other, nay! in one's own solitary self-pity, *even*

Third edition

There have been occasions, certainly, when I have felt that if others cared for me as I *cared* for them, it would be, not so much a *consolation,* as an equivalent, for *what one has lost or suffered: a realised profit on the summing up of one's accounts:* a touching of that absolute ground *amid* all the changes of phenomena, such as our philosophers *have of late confessed* themselves quite unable to *discover.* In the mere clinging of human crea-

amidst what might seem absolute loss,
I seem to touch the eternal.

Vol. II, p. 204, 1. 10

tures to each other, nay! in one's
own solitary self-pity, *amid the effects
even of what might appear irredee-
mable* loss, I seem to touch the eternal.

Vol. II, p. 202, 1. 3

Many of the variations between the texts are so intricate — a change
of word, for instance, coupled with a change in the word order — that
any attempt to enumerate the total number of variations must vary
according to the definition of a variation. It was found useful when
collating the texts to classify the variations into the following thirteen
categories:

Alterations of words and phrases
1. Change of a particular word or phrase
2. Change in the word order
3. Addition of words or phrases
4. Omission ”   ”   ”   ”

Alterations of punctuation
5. Change of Punctuation
6. Omission   ”
7. Addition   ”

Miscellaneous
8. Avoidance of sentences beginning "It was ..."
9. Change in tense
10. Change of sentence construction
11. Creation of new paragraph
12. Elucidation of foreign words and phrases
13. Revision affecting meaning

These categories were formed empirically, and are not intended to be
exclusive of each other. Thus category 8 can usually be included in 1 or 4;
category 9 in 1; and category 12 in 3. The only category that is meant
to be exclusive is the last one: all variations that involve any change in
the meaning have been relegated to this section, whichever of the previous
twelve they may otherwise belong to.

It may be useful at this stage, in order to give a sense of perspective,
to quote the figures of the number of alterations found on this classification. As against the total number of words in the whole work of nearly
120,000, the number of variations between the texts of the first three

editions was 6,085. And the numbers for each of the categories mentioned above are as follows:

1.	Change of a particular word or phrase	2,066
2.	Change in the word order	249
3.	Addition of words or phrases	596
4.	Omission of ” ”	406
5.	Change of punctuation	788
6.	Omission ”	1,358
7.	Addition ”	371
8.	Avoidance of sentence beginning "It was"	59
9.	Change of tense	40
10.	Change of sentence construction	100
11.	Creation of new paragraph	3
12.	Elucidation of foreign words and phrases	16
13.	Revision affecting meaning	33

It is notable that 2,517 variations, or over 40 % of the total, represent changes in punctuation alone, half of them omissions. Of the rest, the number of changes in sentence construction is only 100, most of which are but technical (as when a dash or colon is replaced by a full-stop), and the number of revisions affecting meaning only 33. It must be added at once, however, that this last figure refers sometimes to passages of a page or more in the original, and where the revision is so extensive and fundamental that any detailed breaking down would be superfluous. The whole passage has therefore been regarded as one change in meaning.

It is proposed to describe as completely as possible all the significant changes I have found in the textual history of *Marius the Epicurean*, and to give an impression of the extent and occurrence of the remainder. Since the number of sentences in the first and second editions which, apart from the two passages mentioned, remain unaltered in any way in the third edition is very small, and since nearly every sentence in the work contains examples from several of the categories which have been made, I think that the most economical and least confusing method of presenting them is by the categories themselves, rather then chapter by chapter. In using this method, moreover, the changes in punctuation, which bulk so largely in the total number of changes in the text, as well as the occasional changes in tense, can adequately be illustrated incidentally by the quotations used for other purposes. As a rule, no comment will therefore be made upon them.

A   Change of a particular word or phrase.

It will be noticed among the figures given that this represents the largest single category of variations, over a third of the total number.

In so far as it is possible to deduce general principles covering the changes in this category, they appear for the most part to have been made for one of the following reasons:

I) to give a more concrete image when something is being described;

II) to make the idea being presented more definite and exact;

III) to avoid an obvious or hackneyed expression;

IV) to avoid an unfortunate assonance or alliteration; or

V) to achieve a better rhythm and cadence.

The following examples will perhaps illustrate these points more clearly. (The words and phrases which are peculiar to each edition are again, for convenience, italicised.)

A lad was just then drawing the water for *temple* uses, and Marius followed him as he returned from the well, more and more impressed by the religiousness of all he saw, *as he passed* through a long *corridor*, the walls *of which were well-nigh covered by* votive inscriptions recording favours received from the son of Apollo, and with a *lurking* fragrance of incense in the air, explained, *as* he turned aside through an open doorway into the temple itself.

1st ed., Vol. I, p. 39, 1. 23

A lad was just then drawing water for *ritual* uses, and Marius followed him as he returned from the well, more and more impressed by the religiousness of all he saw *on his way* through a long *cloister or corridor*, the walls *well-nigh hidden under* votive inscriptions recording favours from the son of Apollo, and with *a distant* fragrance of incense in the air, explained *when* he turned aside through an open doorway into the temple itself.

3rd ed., Vol. I, p. 39, 1. 25

In this descriptive sentence, the noun-adjective "temple" is rejected for the more precise "ritual" and because it occurs again at the end of the sentence; "corridor" is replaced by "cloister or corridor" to give a sharper mental picture; the phrase "the walls of which were well-nigh covered by" reduced to the simpler "the walls well-nigh hidden under"; and the obvious qualification "lurking" applied to "fragrance" changed to the more unusual and striking "distant". This sentence illustrates (I) and (III) above.

While all their heart was in their limited boyish race, and its transitory prizes, he was already, in a great measure, entertaining himself, *in a very pleasurable meditativeness*, on the *little*

While all their heart was in their limited boyish race, and its transitory prizes, he was already entertaining himself, *very pleasurably meditative*, with the *tiny* drama in action before drama in action before him, as but the mimic, preliminary exercise for a larger contest; and already with an implicit Epicureanism.

I 49 I. 20

him, as but the mimic, preliminary exercise for a larger contest, and already with an implicit epicureanism.

I 49 1. 22

Here the diffuse and awkward "in a very pleasurable meditativeness" is reduced to the simpler and more direct "very pleasurably meditative", giving a sharper impression to the thought of the sentence. The more obvious "little drama" is changed to the unusual "tiny drama". These illustrate (II) and (III) above.

So, little by little, they stole upon the *soul* of their sister.

I 77 1. 16

So, little by little they stole upon the *heart* of their sister.

I 78 1. 5

By changing "soul" to "heart" Pater at the same time chooses the more appropriate word and avoids the alliteration and assonance of "stole upon the soul of their sister". This illustrates (IV).

First of all, the master of ceremonies and his marshals, quietly waving back the crowd, made way for a number of women, who scattered flowers and perfumes.

I 114 1. 4

At the head of the procession the master of ceremonies, quietly waving back the assistants, made way for a number of women scattering perfumes.

I 114 1. 5

This sentence is re-cast, but without altering the meaning in any very material way. The five clauses of the first version, which give a broken, staccato effect, are reduced to three, giving an easier flow to the sentence as a whole, a rhythm and cadence, and consequently also a clearer impression of the meaning. This illustrates (V).

These five general principles cover the majority of changes in this category, but there are a number of changes that, as well as further illustrating them, are interesting enough in themselves to be given in detail. The following appear to be the more important of these, taken in the order in which they occur in the book:

There was a tone of *reserved gravity* there, amid perfectly disciplined health, which, to his fancy, *carried on* the expression of the austere *light*, and the clear song of the blackbird, on that grey March evening.

I 53 1. 5

There was a tone of *reserve or gravity* there, amid perfectly disciplined health, which, to his fancy, *seemed to carry forward* the expression of the austere *sky* and the clear song of the blackbird on that gray March evening.

I 53 1. 8

The clarity achieved by the revision of the opening clause, by the simple substitution of "reserve or gravity" for the somewhat pleonastic "reserved gravity", is a good example of the more exact expression that Pater tried to achieve. The first version contains just that slightly confused expression that he consistently detects and amends: the thought of the original in no way being altered or extended except so far as is necessary to make the idea more precise. In addition, the alterations to the punctuation considerably improve the rhythm of the sentence.

As throughout the third edition, the spelling of the word "grey", one of Pater's favourite words, is altered to "gray".

It was a strange notion of the *coarse* lust of the actual world, *which Marius got* from some of these episodes.	It was a strange notion of the *gross* lust of the actual world *that Marius took* from some of these episodes.
I 65 1. 9	I 65 1. 13

This sentence is interesting in that Pater, in choosing "gross" rather than "coarse" to qualify "lust", accepts the common phrase as being undoubtedly the more precise. On the other hand, "got" follows the fate of many other colloquial words and phrases in the first edition and is changed to "took". Since the verb "to get" can rarely be used precisely, this sentence shows that Pater by no means rejects a colloquial expression as such, but continues to use the test of precision as his criterion.

There are also other examples in the third text where the more limiting particle "that" is preferred, as here, to "which". Particles are very frequently altered (or rather removed) in the revision, but it is perhaps odd that Pater should have used the particle "which" in the first place here at all.

His dilettantism, his assiduous pre-occupation with what might seem *but the details of mere form or manner, was,* after all, *bent upon the function* of bringing to the surface, sincerely and in their integrity, certain strong personal intuitions, ...	*That pre-occupation of the dilettante* with what might seem *mere details of form,* after all *did but serve the purpose* of bringing to the surface, sincerely and in their integrity, certain strong personal intuitions, ...
I 110 1. 19	I 110 1. 21

Simplification and precision of thought is the purpose of the revision here, and there can be no doubt that the version of the third edition is superior. Apart from the transfer of "mere" to its correct reference, the thought is made clearer by the elimination of the unnecessary words "assiduous" and "manner", and the substitution of the confused "bent upon the function" by "serve the purpose". The revised version has a smoothness and rhythm not possessed by the first.

On the preceding night, all the world had been abroad to view the illumination of the river; the stately lines of *houses on its shores* being *festooned* with hundreds of many-coloured lamps.	*On the evening next before,* all the world had been abroad to view the illumination of the river; the stately lines of *building* being *wreathed* with hundreds of many-coloured lamps.
I 113, 1. 4	I 113 1. 5

The kind of alteration and omission illustrated by this sentence does not often occur. Except for the substitution of the more accurate "evening" for "night", it is difficult to feel that the revised opening phrase is not inferior and more ungainly than the first version. Similarly, the substitution of the more general "building" for "houses on its shores", no doubt because the latter phrase is already implicit in the context, removes a detail of description that only takes away from the image. Pater ignores the fact that readers are in the habit of passing over descriptions more rapidly than passages demanding some concentration, and that they are therefore grateful for such detail. Finally, the word "wreathed", another favourite of Pater's, carries associations that are out of place, and is surely less precise, than the original "festooned".

At this time, *with his* inward and poetic temper, he might have fallen a prey to the enervating mysticism *which was then lying* in wait for ardent souls, in many a melodramatic revival of old religion or theosophy. From all that, *attractive as it might* be to one side of his nature, he was kept by *his real virility — by something well-braced or cynical even* — effective in him, among other results, as a hatred *of theatricality,* and an instinctive recognition that in vigorous intelligence *must be indeed the most real presence of the divine being.*	At this time, *by his* poetic and inward temper, he might have fallen a prey to the enervating mysticism, *then* in wait for ardent souls in many a melodramatic revival of old religion or theosophy. From all this, *fascinating as it might actually* be to one side of his character, he was *kept by a genuine virility there,* effective in him, among other results, as a hatred *of what was theatrical,* and the instinctive recognition that in vigorous intelligence, *after all, divinity was most likely to be found a resident.*
I 134 1. 10	I 134 1. 11

There can be little doubt of the success of the revision here. The diffuseness and hesitancy of the first edition is eliminated, every alteration made being apt and, with the final phrase, even striking. The rhythm of the sentences is also improved.

The bold, *pantheistic* flight of the old Greek master from the *fleeting object* to that one universal life, in which the whole sphere of physical change might be reckoned but as a single pulsation, remained by him but as a hypothesis only — the hypothesis he actually preferred, as in itself most credible, however scantily realisable even by the imagination — yet still but as one unverified hypothesis, concerning the first principle of things, among many others.

I 143 1. 1

The bold *mental* flight of the old Greek master from *the fleeting, competing, objects of experience* to that one universal life, in which the whole sphere of physical change might be reckoned as but a single pulsation, remained by him as hypothesis only — the hypothesis he actually preferred, as in itself most credible, however scantily realisable even by the imagination — yet still as but one unverified hypothesis among many others concerning the first principle of things.

I 143 1. 6

The only change that, I feel, can be called into question in this sentence is the substitution of the somewhat more accurate but certainly less colourful "mental" for "pantheistic". The alteration of "fleeting object" to "fleeting, competing, objects of experience" gains precision and achieves an almost poetic rhythm. The changes in word and clause order in the final part of the sentence combine to produce a perfect rounded sentence.

And just here he joined company, retracing in his *intellectual* pilgrimage the *actual* historic order of *old philosophy*, with another wayfarer on the journey, another ancient Greek master, the founder of the Cyrenaic philosophy, whose *impressive*, traditional utterances (for he had left no writing) served, in turn, to give effective outline to *his thoughts*.

I 144 1. 19

Just here he joined company, retracing in his *individual mental* pilgrimage the historic order of *human thought*, with another wayfarer on the journey, another ancient Greek master, the founder of the Cyrenaic philosophy, whose *weighty* traditional utterances (for he had left no writing) served in turn to give effective outline to *the contemplations of Marius*.

I 144 1. 26

It is especially this kind of sentence, which, because it is so close to the central theme of the book necessarily occurs frequently, Pater is most at pains to improve. Three words in the first edition — 'intellectual', 'philosophy' and 'thoughts' — he alters or varies as often as possible: they are abstract words of course, but Pater is also aware of their tendency to recur, and for this reason changes them sometimes irrespective of whether a better effect is achieved. Thus here, although 'philosophy' and 'thoughts' are successfully circumvented, it is difficult to feel that "individual mental pilgrimage" is in any way preferable to "intellectual pilgrimage".

Wherever possible, again, Pater removes the word 'and' when it begins a sentence. As it is usually redundant, it is only retained when it acts as a necessary rhythmic bridge between two sentences.

It seemed just then as if the desire of the artist in him — that old longing to produce — might be satisfied by the exact and *just expression merely* of what was then passing around him, in simple prose, ... I 177 1. 5

It seemed just then as if the desire of the artist in him — that old longing to produce — might be satisfied by the exact and *literal transcript* of what was then passing around him, in simple prose, ... I 179 1. 12

Apart from being more precise, it is interesting that the phrase preferred in the third edition is taken from the essay on "Style". — Perhaps the thoughts suggested by the writing of the essay are also responsible for the dropping of the derogatory "merely".

Many a Roman courtier agreed with the barbarian chief, who, after contemplating *one of the predecessors* of Aurelius, withdrew from his presence with the exclamation — "I have seen *Gods* today!" I 230 1. 19

Many a Roman courtier agreed with the barbarian chief, who, after contemplating *a predecessor* of Aurelius, withdrew from his presence with the exclamation: — "I have seen *a god* today!" I 234 1. 24

With such emendations as these, it is possible that the desire to simplify the text has over-reached itself; the gain in brevity in the revised version can scarcely be said to compensate the loss of the rhythm and dramatic effect of the earlier version.

And still, all the while, he *allows* no moral world as such; *real though it be to Aeschylus, to Socrates, to Virgil: as also to a thousand commonplace souls.*

II 9 1. 12

And yet all the while he *admits*, as such, no moral world at all: *no theoretic equivalent to so large a proportion of the facts of life.*

II 9 1. 12

The latter part of this sentence qualifies, of course, the abstract phrase "moral world", and it is interesting that whereas Pater chooses to illustrate this in the first version by particular examples, he prefers in the third version to keep the thought on an abstract level. It is difficult to feel that the latter does in fact help to clarify the thought.

Behind their light trelliswork, Marius watched the riders, arrayed in all their gleaming ornaments, and wearing *chaplets* of olive *round* their *casques;* the faces below which, what with pla-

Through that light trelliswork, Marius watched the riders arrayed in all their gleaming ornaments, and wearing *wreaths* of olive *around* their *helmets,* the faces below which, what with

gue and battle, were *nearly* all youthful.

II 13 1. 20

battle and the plague, were *almost* all
youthful.

II 13 1. 22

Apart from the interesting rejection of the archaic "chaplets" and "casques", the changes in this sentence are, typically, dictated by internal reasons. Thus the opening words are changed in order to eliminate the least
important of the three "their"'s in the sentence; the transposition of
"plague" and "battle" adds to the euphony; and "almost all" for "nearly
all" gives another lengthened syllable such as Pater is so fond of for
cadence.

And for his part he has *made his
choice* and *is true to it.*

II 57 1. 18

For his part he has *asserted his will,*
and *has the courage of his position.*

II 53 1. 1

This example is given as one of the occasional instances where the will
to be precise has sacrificed a desirable simplicity. It is interesting that the
criterion of precision should have first place: for it is impossible to deny
that the direct statement of the first edition is superior to the awkward
and prolix alternative.

When Marius recalled *it,* he seemed
always to hear *again the* voice of
genuine conviction, from amidst *that*
scene of at best elegant frivolity,
pleading for so boldly mystical a view
of *things.*

II 103 1. 6

When Marius recalled *its circumstances* he seemed to hear *once more
that* voice of genuine conviction, pleading, from amidst *a* scene at best of
elegant frivolity, for so boldly mystical a view of *man and his position in
the world.*

II 97 1. 8

The more important changes here illustrate Pater's general concern
to avoid too great a degree of abstraction. Thus in the opening phrase,
"it" is expanded to its reference, and the vague final phrase given a
somewhat more exact meaning. Almost all the changes of this nature do
in fact help to clarify the meaning.

The ritual system of the church,
which must rank as we see it in historic retrospect, like the Gothic architecture for instance, as one of the
great, conjoint and, so to term them,
necessary, products of human mind,
and which has ever since directed, with
so deep a fascination, men's religious
instincts, was then growing together,

Like the institutions of monasticism,
like the Gothic style of architecture,
the ritual system of the church, as we
see it in historic retrospect, ranks as
one of the great conjoint and (so to
term them) necessary, products of human mind. Destined for ages to come,
to direct with so deep a fascination
men's religious instincts, it was then

as a recognisable new treasure in the sum of things. II 139 1. 26	already recognisable as a new and precious fact in the sum of things. II 135 1. 3

The many verbal changes in this passage are not, ultimately, as important as the rearrangement and splitting of the sentence, but it is given here to illustrate how often the changes in word order and clause order entail changes in particular words also, sometimes demanded as much by euphony as by desire to be more exact. The version of the third edition is immeasurably superior to the halting first one.

In addition to the quotations already given, the following phrases may perhaps be taken without undue strain from their contexts to illustrate a happier and more effective word change when something is being described. The line reference in the first column is to the first edition:

	First edition	*Third edition*
I 39 1. 5	just full to the margin	full to the brim
52 1. 24	the distinction of his broad smooth forehead	the distinction of the low, broad forehead
118 1. 16	this sudden heat of spring	this sudden spasm of spring
120 1. 11	Flavian lay at the open window of his lodging, with a burning pain in the head	Flavian lay at the open window of his lodging, with a fiery pang in the brain
161 1. 26	Marius was still pure and strong.	The blood, the heart of Marius was still pure.
169 1. 3	He acquired at this time a certain bookishness	He acquired at this time a certain bookish air
175 1. 24	Nature, under the richer sky, seemed readier and more affluent and man fitter to his circumstances.	Nature, under the richer sky, seemed readier and more affluent, and man fitter to the conditions around him.
II 6 1. 6	a vocabulary which rejected every term and phrase not stamped with the authority of the most approved ancient models.	a vocabulary which rejected every expression unsanctioned by the authority of approved ancient models.

The following similar quotations are intended to illustrate changes which present thought more sharply and exactly:

		First edition	Third edition
I	50 1. 22	That apprehension had come upon him very strongly one exceptionally fine summer	That sense had come upon him in all its power one exceptionally fine summer
	51 1. 7	a boundless appetite for experience, for material and spiritual adventure.	a boundless appetite for experience, for adventure, whether physical or of the spirit.
	117 1. 8	the very strain which Flavian had caught back in those last months.	the very strain which Flavian had recovered in those last months.
	158 1. 13	as defining the true limits	as ascertaining the true limits
	165 1. 16	Though he had changed, formally, from poetry to prose, he was still, and must always be, of the poetic temper	Though the manner of his work was changed formally from poetry to prose, he remained, and must always be, of the poetic temper
II	8 1. 2	He supposed his hearer to be sincerely in search of a practical principle	He supposed his hearer to be, with all sincerity, in search after some principle of conduct
	114 1. 22	All criticism of this bold hope	All critical estimate of this bold hope
	150 1. 4	In the old pagan worship there had been little to call out the intelligence.	In the old pagan worship there had been little to call the understanding into play.

It is also possible to give the following list of changes in single words showing the trend to choose a more particular and limited word for the third edition:

First edition		Third edition
order	becomes	ritual
main		chief
constitution		being
carefully		punctiliously
procession		pageant
victor		conqueror
religious		pious
quarter		neighbourhood
thought		reasoning

Against this, however, there is a tendency for this principle, especially when applied to concrete descriptions of things and people, to produce an outlandish, sometimes almost obsolete word. Thus:

First edition		Third edition
flowers	becomes	garlands
flowers		blossom
grass		verdure
streets		thoroughfares
complain		repine
wintry		dusky
surrounded		encircled
house		abode
noble		patrician
criminal		wrong-doer

In this connection, it may be mentioned that at one point Pater changes "cedar" (as adjective) to the archaic and poetical "cedarn". Generally, however, Pater is always at trouble in the revision of *Marius* to remove his own verbal excesses, as when "abstractedness" becomes just "abstraction", "divinised" becomes "deified", and "reconcilement" becomes "reconciliation".

Finally, there is one strange error in the first edition which might conveniently be mentioned here:

> "What more ingenious diversion had stage-manager ever contrived than that incident, itself a practical epigram never to be forgotten, when a criminal, who, like slaves and animals, had no rights, was compelled to present the part of Daedalus; and, the wings failing him in due course, had fallen among a crowd of hungry bears."   I 256 1. 9

"Daedalus" is changed to "Icarus" in the second and all subsequent editions.

By way of summarising this category, I think there are no particularly remarkable trends, apart from the five general principles given at first, to be observed in the alterations to words and phrases. What is perhaps surprising is that no specific word or phrase occuring in the first edition is invariably proscribed in the later editions: that is, the changes have clearly been made from principle only. Although it is true that Pater was particularly concerned with avoiding abstract words wherever possible, this is due to the central theme of the book perhaps as much as any conscious and deliberate intention to avoid such words in themselves.

Enough examples have been quoted to be able to say, at this stage, that in spite of the few occasions when they are not successful, the majority of the changes are happy in producing a sharper impression, neater outline and a finer rhythm. Where the changes are noticably for the worse it is observed that they usually occur, strangely, in the more explicitly descriptive passages.

B   *Changes in the word order*

In view of the care Pater had for the construction of his sentences, and his extremely delicate ear for their rhythm, it is perhaps remarkable that in this category only 249 examples, many of them trivial, have been noted in the revision of so long a work.

The changes present a relatively simple pattern. Invariably there is an attempt to improve rhythm and euphony, but coupled with this the device is frequently used in order to reduce the number of parts or clauses in a sentence. Generally, the changes made are very successful and there is only a small number where it is difficult to see that any advantage has been obtained.

The extent of the particular changes included in this category varies considerably. Pater is fondest of the simple transposition of two nouns or adjectives standing in the same grammatical relationship, and in point of fact it is this kind of change for which sometimes it is most difficult to see justification. When the changes involve the rearrangement of the whole sentence, however, the improvement in rhythm, and especially cadence, is usually striking.

The following, given in the order in which they occur, are examples of simple rearrangement or transposition of words where the improvement in rhythm is easily noticeable:

		First edition	Third edition
I	47 1.19	The pensive, partly decayed place	The partly decayed, pensive town
	48 1.25	the house of his tutor or guardian	the home of his guardian or tutor
	50 1.19	down even to its little passing tricks of fashion	down to its little passing tricks of fashion even
	77 1.9	But the sisters made their way once more into the palace	But the sisters make their way into the palace once more
	111 1.23	Certainly it is the most typical expression of a mood	It is certainly the most typical expression of a mood

135	1.11	the results of the honest action of his own unassisted, untroubled intelligence.	the honest action of his own untroubled, unassisted intelligence.
136	1.9	He came of age at this time, though with beardless face, his own master;	He came of age about this time, his own master though with beardless face;
149	1.16	like the little waves and knots in a mirror	like the little knots and waves in a mirror
153	1.1	this hard, bold, sober recognition	this bold, hard, sober recognition
157	1.2	the heaviness and vulgarity of a generation	the vulgarity and heaviness of a generation
158	1.18	the powers of sensation and emotion.	the powers of emotion and sense.
175	1.6	exaggerating every circumstance and symptom of misery	exaggerating every symptom and circumstance of misery
181	1.20	a very austere and grave, kind of beauty	a very grave and austere, kind of beauty
190	1.20	from which Lucius Verus had brought back the plague among other curiosities,	from which Lucius Verus among other curiosities brought back the plague,
215	1.2	The world without and within me	The world within me and without
235	1.7	men's and women's eternal shortcomings.	the eternal shortcomings of men and women.
253	1.4	a trellis-work of amber and silver-gilt	a trellis-work of silver-gilt and amber
II 72	1.5	things so fine also in material and workmanship	things so fine also in workmanship and material
76	1.2	under its broad, shadowless light every tone and hue of time came out upon the old yellow temples	under its broad, shadowless light every hue and tone of time came out upon the yellow old temple
99	1.20	Pausing on the terrace for a few minutes to watch it	Pausing for a few minutes on the terrace to watch it
136	1.14	that it may live in what survives the more completely;	that it may live the more completely in what survives of it;
148	1.24	repeated again and again alternately,	repeated alternately, again and again,
190	1.7	There seemed to Marius to be some new meaning	To Marius there seemed to be some new meaning

II 216 1. 15	that there might be not a ve-stige of them left upon the earth.	that not a vestige of them might be left upon the earth.

The following examples of changes in word order are like the preceding ones in showing an improvement in rhythm, but in addition it will be noted that as a result of the change two clauses have been run into one:

I 38 1. 10	an inscription in letters of gold, which ran round the base of the cupola, recorded it	an inscription around the cu-pola recorded it in letters of gold
96 1. 12	And Cupid, his wound being now healed,	And Cupid being healed of his wound,
114 1. 7	They were followed by a com-pany of musicians, twanging and piping,	They were succeeded by a company of musicians piping and twanging,
II 151 1. 16	having reference to a power still efficacious, and in action among the people there as-sembled, in some mystic sense.	having reference to a power still efficacious, still after so-me mystic sense even now in action among the people there assembled.
246 1. 4	Of old, he had often fancied	Often he had fancied of old

The reason for the change in the following example, however, is not so clear:

I 23 1. 20	It fixed in him a sympathy for all creatures, for the al-most human sicknesses and troubles of the flocks, for in-stance.	It fixed in him a sympathy for all creatures, for the almost human troubles and sicknesses of the flocks, for instance.

Although it may be said that the rhythm is slightly improved, surely here the revised "sickness of the flocks, for instance" produces an un-fortunate agglomeration of 's' sounds!

Similarly, I feel that in each of the following instances the revised version is inferior to the original one:

I 137 1. 6	the distant haunted horizon of mere imagination or surmise	the distant, haunted horizon of mere surmise or imagination
140 1. 11	not as a stagnant and sterile inaction	not as a sterile and stagnant inaction
204 1. 13	an expression of effort and fatigue	an expression of fatigue and effort

II 82 1.11	Himself — his ideas and sensations — never fell again precisely into focus as on that day	Himself — his sensations and ideas — never fell again precisely into focus as on that day
120 1.8	one of his most constant and characteristic traits	one of his most characteristic and constant traits
190 1.2	to rifle some ruined or neglected tomb	to rifle some neglected or ruined tomb

And finally, the following are the instances where whole sentences have been rearranged or recast. In each case there is a distinct gain in rhythm and shape:

I 187 1.9	So, the grave, pensive figure, a figure far fresher than often came across it now, moved through the old city, certainly not by the most direct course, though eager to join the friend of yesterday, to the lodgings of Cornelius.	So the grave pensive figure, a figure, be it said, nevertheless, fresher far than often came across it now, moved through the old city towards the lodgings of Cornelius, certainly not by the most direct course, however eager to join the friend of yesterday.
189 1.4	He exerted for that function a strength of voice which confirmed in Marius a judgment, the modern visitor may share with him, and which he had formed in part the night before, noting as a religious procession passed him, how much noise a man and a boy could make, though not without a great deal of real music, of which, indeed, the Romans were then as ever passionately fond — the judgment, namely, that Roman throats and chests must, in some particular way, be differently constructed from those of other people.	He exerted for this function a strength of voice, which confirmed in Marius a judgment the modern visitor may share with him, that Roman throats and chests, namely, must, in some peculiar way, be differently constructed from those of other people. Such judgment indeed he had formed in part the evening before, noting, as a religious procession passed him, how much noise a man and a boy could make, though not without a great deal of real music, of which in truth the Romans were then as ever passionately fond.
236 1.14	"I, for my part, unless I conceive my hurt as such, have no hurt at all."	"For my part, unless I conceive my hurt to be such, I have no hurt at all."
II 10 1.7	There was one great idea (Fronto proceeded to expound the idea of humanity — of a	There was one great idea, associated with which that determination to conform to

universal commonwealth of minds — which yet somehow becomes conscious, and as if incarnate, in a select body of just men made perfect) in association with which the determination to conform to precedent was elevated into the weightiest, the fullest, the clearest principle of moral action; a principle under which one might subsume men's most strenuous efforts after righteousness.

precedent was elevated into the clearest, the fullest, the weightiest principle of moral action; a principle under which one might subsume men's most strenuous efforts after righteousness. And he proceeded to expound the idea of Humanity — of a universal commonwealth of mind, which becomes explicit, and as if incarnate, in a select communion of just men made perfect.

Virtually all the changes in word order, then, whether they consist of the transposition of two single words or amount to a total rearrangement of a sentence, can be regarded as successful. The changes in the order of single words appear to have as their first intention an improvement in rhythm and euphony, though these qualities of course have at least negative value in clarifying the meaning also. The sound, that is, is not allowed to be a barrier to sense. And this point is amply reinforced in the changes in word order on a larger scale, where the improvement in both rhythm and impact is considerable.

C   *Omissions of words and phrases*

When revising the text of *Marius the Epicurean*, Pater took the opportunity to eliminate from the first and second editions many single words and phrases that he regarded as unnecessary. It must be said at once, however, that few of these deletions can be described as obvious: they are of value principally as indicating the extremely rigorous standards that Pater held in mind when revising the text. The determination he shows in removing any words not directly and explicitly contributing to the sense, and any detail that might be thought irrelevant, can only be called ruthless.

Again it is important to note that rarely is the thought in any material way altered or suppressed as a result of these changes. The alterations included in this category show once more that his object was to present the original thought more lucidly and exactly.

Any words which savour of repetition or pleonasm are, of course, invariably suppressed. In descriptions, also, Pater removes any details that are already otherwise implied in the context, and any tending towards the pedantic. He ferociously excludes words bordering on cliché, and shows a particular anxiety to suppress unnecessary particles. And finally, as though becoming more conscious of his habit of qualification, there are a few instances of where this is deleted also.

Of the 406 examples noted in this category, many, particularly the suppression of particles, are of course trivial, and the following quotations are offered as the most generally representative. The text given is that of the first edition, with the words removed in the third edition italicised.

Removal of repetition

Consider how quickly all things vanish away — their bodily structure into the general substance *of things;* the very memory of them into that great gulf and abysm of past thoughts. Ah! 'tis on a tiny space of earth thou art creeping through life — a pigmy soul carrying a dead body to its grave. *Consider all this with thyself, and let nothing seem great to thee.*   I 220 1. 6

the "following of the reasonable will *and ordinance* of the oldest, the most venerable, of all cities and polities — *the reasonable will* of the royal, the lawgiving element in it —   II 11 1. 7

he must for his own peace adjust *and relate* himself?
                    II 13 1. 5

that clear-eyed intellectual *integrity or* consistency, which is like spotless bodily cleanliness *and nicety* or scrupulous personal honour;
                    II 17 1. 16

his capacities *namely* of feeling, of *receiving* exquisite physical impressions,   II 31 1. 1

Purified, as all such religion of concrete time and place needs to be *purified,*   II 50 1. 7

Through a dreamy land he could see himself moving, as if in another life, *detached from the present,* and like another person,
                    II 77 1. 10

Omission of pleonasm

their masters in the art of *correct* thinking   I 162 1. 23

with men of his *chosen* vocation,   I 167 1. 3

A legitimate popular hatred   II 41 1. 18

Removal of detail already implied in the context

Around the walls, ... ran a series of imageries, *carved* in low relief,

I 40 1. 18

he had written for Latin people in their own tongue; though still, in truth, with all the care of *one writing* a learned language.

I 61 1. 13

some of them with long ivory combs, plying their hands *and decking their hair,*

I 114 1. 16

in the wake of a much stouter vessel than itself, *manned by a crew* of white-robed mariners,

I 116 1. 5

yet concentrating within it an epitome of all that was liveliest.

I 117 1. 16

she had gone out to him at Ephesus and become his wife by the form of civil marriage, the more solemn wedding rites being deferred till the return *of the bride and bridegroom* to Rome.

I 247 1. 12

with the hushed footsteps of people who move about a house *of mourning* where a dead body is lying.

II 59 1. 13

predecessor, under the patronage of Aesculapius, to the modern hospital for the sick on the island of Saint Bartholomew *in the Tiber.*

II 127 1. 1

Removal of detail regarded as unnecessary

Marius was one of the most eager, deeply interested in finding the spectacle much as Apuleius had described it in his book, *though on a scale less grand.*

I 113 1. 26

a choir of *white-vested* youths,

I 114 1. 11

the *old yellow* marble of its villas glittering all the way

II 73 1. 22

Removal of pedantic detail

How reassuring, after *assisting at* so long a debate

I 149 1. 26

It was in the actions of one person that the whole mystery centred. Distinguished among his assistants, who stood ranged in semicircle around him *(themselves parted from the general congregation by transennae, or lattice-work, of pierced white marble)* by the extreme fineness or whiteness of his vesture, and the pointed cap with golden ornaments on his head, *this person, nevertheless, struck Marius as*

*having something about him like one of the wild shepherds of the
Campagna.*   II 151 1. 26

The table or altar at which he presided, below a canopy of spiral
columns, *and with the carved palm-branch, standing in the midst of a
semicircle of seats for the priests,* was in reality the tomb of a youthful
"witness",   II 152 1. 26

Removal of cliché or hackneyed word
Through the *yawning* breach a rough way lies open,
                                                      I 93 1. 25

A *blind* feeling of outrage,
                                                      I 128 1. 2

determined partly by *purely* natural affection,
                                                      II 8 1. 7

Removal of particles
remained by him *but* as *a* hypothesis only —
                                                      I 143 1. 5

But then, on the other hand,
                                                      I 160 1. 1

The torches *which had been* made ready to do him a useless honour
were of real service now,
                                                      I 225 1. 17

anniversary of the victory of *the* Lake Regillus
                                                      II 13 1. 16

Removal of qualification
The popular speech was gradually departing from the form and rule
of literary language, a language always and increasingly *somewhat*
artificial.   I 102 1. 3

Here and there, an *actual* funeral procession was slowly on its way,
in weird contrast to the gaiety of the hour.
                                                      II 159 1. 21

I saw today, under one of the archways of the baths, two children very
seriously at play — a fair girl and a *perfectly* crippled younger brother.
                                                      II 201 1. 23

While the reasons for the deletions are clear, it can easily be felt that
the pursuit of a principle has here been taken too far. It is doubtful, for
instance, whether the closely-knit and tightly fitting style Pater is aiming
at, is appropriate to such an extended narrative; or if it is appropriate,
whether some relaxation of the tautness might not on occasion give a use-

ful relief — particularly, of course, in descriptive passages. And though it is true that the words and phrases deleted do not, for the most part, add to the thought, they do nevertheless help to sharpen or emphasise some aspect that is otherwise neglected in the sentence. This consideration Pater, with a dread of 'padding', does not countenance, and I feel that in the majority of instances in this category the omission is not, on larger grounds, justified.

D   *Addition of words and phrases*

In the classification adopted there are in fact more instances of addition of words and phrases in the third edition of *Marius the Epicurean* than there are of omission — 596, as against 406. The majority of the additions are in the way of the filling out of a thought or a description which might possibly be obscure as it stands in the first edition, and it cannot often be disputed that they serve a useful purpose.

Inevitably, from the nature of the book, the elaboration of a particular line of thought represents the largest single number of additions made to the third text. But there are a small number of instances where Pater, more aware perhaps of the lack of imagery — what might be called the picture value of his novel — adds small details of description, in an attempt to present a more concrete and vivid scene.

A very small number of words seem most probably to have been added primarily for rhythmical reasons, to give euphony or cadence. And a similarly small number show his innate habit of qualification asserting itself over a too broad statement in the first text.

Finally, there is a group where the reason for the addition is obscure in that they are additions of detail precisely of a kind already noted as being consistently removed when they occur in the first edition.

General examples of where a particular train of thought as expressed in the first text is expanded in a successful attempt at greater definition, are as follows. (Where one text only is given it is that of the third edition, the words peculiar to either edition again being italicised.)

Were they doctrines one might take for granted, generously take for granted — and led along by them, at first as but well-defined *hopes, grow at last into the corresponding intellectual certitude?*　II 74 1. 13	Were they doctrines one might take for granted, generously take for granted, and led on by them, at first as but well-defined *objects of hope, come at last into the region of a corresponding certitude of the intellect?*　II 70 1. 2

How often had the recollection of their transitoriness spoiled *his* most natural pleasures in life, actually confusing his sense of them by a suggestion *of failure and death in everything!*

II 81 1. 11

How often had the thought of their brevity spoiled *for him the* most natural pleasures of life, confusing even his *present* sense of them by the suggestion *of disease, of death, of a coming end, in everything!*

II 77 1. 8

And from the first they could hear singing — the singing partly of children, it would seem, and of a new sort; so novel indeed in its effect, *that it carried the memory of Marius back to those old efforts of Flavian to conceive a new poesy.*

II 109 1. 18

And from the first they could hear singing, the singing of children mainly, it would seem, and of a new kind; so novel indeed in its effect, *as to bring suddenly to the recollection of Marius Flavian's early essays towards a new world of poetic sound.*

II 103 1. 25

The stern heart, applying the faulty theology, of John Calvin, afforded him, we know, the vision of infants not a span long, on the floor of hell.

II 115 1. 4

The stern soul *of the excellent Jonathan Edwards,* applying the faulty theology of John Calvin, afforded him, we know, the vision of infants not a span long on the floor of hell.

II 109 1. 17

Notwithstanding the absence of any *definite or central visible image.*

II 151 1. 22

Notwithstanding the absence of any *central image visible to the eye.*

II 147 1. 3

To some, perhaps, the circumstances of my own life may cause me necessarily to be opposed, regarding those interests which actually determine the happiness of theirs.

II 197 1. 21

To some, perhaps, the necessary conditions of my own life may cause me to be opposed, *in a kind of natural conflict* regarding those interests which actually determine the happiness of theirs.

II 195 1. 5

But it had always been his policy, through all his pursuit of "experience", to *fly* in time from any too disturbing passion, likely to quicken his pulses beyond the point at which the quiet work of life was practicable.

II 208 1. 24

But it had always been his policy, through all his pursuit of "experience", to *take flight* in time from any too disturbing passion, *from any sort of affection* likely to quicken his pulses beyond the point at which the quiet work of life was practicable.

II 207 1. 4

The following additions to the text in the third edition no doubt have the intention of presenting a sharper and clearer image:

The sides of the vale lay both alike in full sunlight;　　I 43 1. 17

The *softly sloping* sides of the vale lay alike in full sunlight;　　I 43 1. 21

A heavy tapestry was drawn back;　　I 244 1. 24

A heavy *curtain of* tapestry was drawn back;　　I 249 1. 15

In such wise had Aurelius come to that condition of philosophic detachment, which he had affected as a boy, when he had hardly been persuaded to wear warm clothing, and to sleep otherwise than on the bare floor.

II 43 1. 14

In such wise had Aurelius come to the condition of philosophic detachment he had affected as a boy, hardly persuaded to wear warm clothing, or to sleep *in more luxurious manner* than on the bare floor.　　II 38 1. 15

But it had been, actually, in his clearest vision of it, a confused place, with but a recognisable tower or entry, here or there,　　II 47 1. 26

But it had been actually, in his clearest vision of it, a confused place, with but a recognisable entry, a tower *or fountain*, here or there,

II 42 1. 26

And in the following instances, since no perceptible clarification of thought or image is achieved, the underlined words appear, from the improved rhythm of the sentences, to have been added for this reason only:

To move afterwards in that outer world of other people, as though taking it at their estimate, would be possible *henceforth* only as a kind of irony.　　I 144 1. 12

A strange trick memory sometimes played him; for, with no natural gradation, what was of last month, or of yesterday, *of today even*, would seem as far off, as entirely detached from him, as things of ten years ago.　　I 167 1. 8

The succeeding quotations illustrate some qualification later deemed necessary by Pater to the expression of the first edition. There is no doubt they are justified as a help to clarity:

But what precise place could there be for Verus, and his charm,

I 210 1. 12

But what precise place could there be for Verus and his *peculiar* charm,

I 213 1. 25

(of Marcus Aurelius)
a philosopher whose mystic speculation *surrounded him with a* saintly halo,
I 230 1. 10

a philosopher whose mystic speculation *encircled him with a sort of* saintly halo,　　I 234 1. 14

Hence, his constant circumspection; a close watching of his soul, almost unique in the ancient world —

II 58 1. 25

Hence his constant "recollection"; a close watching of his soul, *of a kind* almost unique in the ancient world.

II 54 1. 8

— But there are occasions when they appear unnecessary:

Certainly, the philosophy of Plato,

II 100 1. 16

Certainly the *contemplative* philosophy of Plato,

II 94 1. 12

I notice *often the true* character of the fondness of the roughest working-people for their young children,

II 201 1. 4

I notice *sometimes what I conceive to be the precise* character of the fondness of the roughest working-people for their young children,

II 198 1. 18

As against all the above, however, the following examples seem perilously close to the kind which has been mentioned as being frequently deleted from the first edition:

a feeling in his case not reminiscent but prescient, which passed over him many times afterwards, coming across certain people and places;

I 122 1. 18

a feeling in his case not reminiscent but prescient *of the future,* which passed over him afterwards many times as he came across certain places and people.

I 122 1. 23

Marius could discern dimly, behind the solemn recitation which now followed (at once a narrative and an invocation or prayer) the most touching image *he had ever beheld.*

II 155 1. 17

Marius could discern dimly, behind the solemn recitation which now followed, at once a narrative and a prayer, the most touching image *truly that had ever come within the scope of his mental or physical gaze.*

II 150 1. 24

And the following examples are of additions of detail that are in fact already fully implied in the text:

as a man might piously stamp on his memory the death-scene of a brother wrongfully condemned, against a time that may come.

I 128 1. 10

as a man might piously stamp on his memory the death-scene of a brother wrongfully condemned *to die,* against a time that may come.

I 128 1. 18

superstitious fear had even demanded a human victim.

I 191 1. 13

superstitious fear had even demanded *the sacrifice of* a human victim.

I 194 1. 11

Hadrian had playfully called him, not Verus, after his father, but Verissimus,	Hadrian had playfully called him, not Verus, after *the name of* his father, but Verissimus,
I 203 1. 17	I 206 1. 20
Righteousness would be, in the words of the Caesar himself,	Righteousness would be, in the words of "Caesar" himself, *of the philosophic Aurelius,*
II 11 1. 6	II 11 1. 7
in the trying atmosphere of intellectual speculation.	in the trying atmosphere of *purely* intellectual vision.
II 50 1. 15	II 45 1. 16

In conclusion, I think it is important to point out that, ruthlessly as Pater deleted words and phrases in the text of the first edition that he later came to feel were unnecessary, he did not hesitate also to add to the text whenever some detail seemed to him inadequately expressed. Behind both the omissions and the additions to the text, therefore, lies equally the primary intention of expressing the thought more precisely and exactly.

E   *Elucidation of foreign words and phrases*

When revising *Marius the Epicurean* for the third edition, Pater adopted a policy of explaining or even removing the more unusual foreign words and phrases that he used in the first edition. There are, in number, sixteen instances of this, and the following are typical examples (the numeral on the left hand side representing the edition):

LATIN

1. Legend told of a visit of Aesculapius to this place, earlier and happier than his first coming to Rome: an inscription in letters of gold, which ran round the base of the cupola, recorded it — *Huc profectus filius Dei maxime amavit hunc locum* — and it was then that this most intimately human of all the gods had given men this well, with all its salutary properties, to be his visible servant or minister.   I 38 1. 8

3. Legend told of a visit of Aesculapius to this place, earlier and happier than his first coming to Rome: an inscription around the cupola recorded it in letters of gold. "Being come unto this place the son of God loved it exceedingly:" —*Huc profectus filius Dei maxime amavit hunc locum;* and it was then that that most intimately human of the gods had given men the well, with all its salutary properties.   I 38 1. 12

1. The image of *Fortuna Muliebris* in the *Via Latina*, had spoken (not once only) and declared; *Bene me matronae vidistis riteque dedicastis.* I 199 1. 3

3. The image of the Fortune of Women — *Fortuna Muliebris*, in the Latin Way, had spoken (not once only) and declared; *Bene me, Matronae! vidistis riteque dedicastis!* I 202 1.4

1. *Hic congesta jacet quaeris si turba piorum:*
   Corpora sanctorum retinet veneranda sepulchra! —

   II 115 1.21

3. Omitted from the third edition

1. The faithful were bent less on the destruction of the pagan temples than on the conversion of them and of their furniture to better uses; and the temples became Christian sanctuaries, with much beautiful furniture ready to hand. II 140 1.19

2. The faithful were bent less on the destruction of the pagan temples than on the conversion of them and of their furniture to better uses; and the temples became Christian sanctuaries, with much beautiful furniture ready to hand. — *In hoc marmore gentilium olim incensa fumabant.* II 127 1. 15

3. The faithful were bent less on the destruction of the old pagan temples than on their conversion to a new and higher use; and, with much beautiful furniture ready to hand, they became Christian sanctuaries. II 135 1. 25

1. *Astiterunt reges terrae* — proceeded the *Sequence*, the young men on the steps of the altar, responding, in deep, clear, antiphon or chorus — II 151 1. 5

3. *Astiterunt reges terrae:* — so the Gradual, the "Song of Degrees," proceeded, the young men on the steps of the altar responding in deep, clear antiphon or chorus — II 146 1. 11

1. Pushing away the grim *fossors*, II 208 1. 14

3. Pushing away the grim *fossores*, the grave-diggers, II 206 1. 19

GREEK

1. In this way, the *becoming*, as the Greeks — or *manners*, as both Greeks and Romans said, would indeed be a comprehensive term for duty. II 11 1. 3

3. In this way, the *becoming*, as in Greek — τὸ πρέπον or πα ηϑη, *mores, manners,* as both Greeks and Romans said, would indeed be a comprehensive term for duty.   II 11 1. 3

1. And there could be no true *Théodicée* in that; no real accomodation of the world as it is to the divine pattern of the *Logos*, over against it.   II 60 1. 5

3. And there could be no true *Théodicée* in that; no real accommodation of the world as it is to the divine pattern of the *Logos*, the eternal reason, over against it.   II 55 1. 15

1. Were there (as the expression ἀναγμαια — *which one could not do without* — seemed to hint) opinions, without which life itself was almost impossible, and which had their sufficient ground of evidence in that fact?   II 74 1. 24

3. Were there, as the expresion *"one could not do without"* seemed to hint, beliefs, without which life itself must be almost impossible, principles which had their sufficient ground of evidence in that very fact?   II 70 1. 15

FRENCH

1. — the cool circle of shadow, in which the wonderful toilets of the *beau monde* told so effectively around the blazing arena.
                    I 252 1. 23

3. the cool circle of shadow in which the wonderful toilets of the fashionable told so effectively around the blazing arena,
                    I 256 1. 26

The third illustration given on page 51, where a Latin phrase is introduced in the second edition and then deleted in the third, is useful in order to emphasise that the changes made for the second text generally are little more than a tidying and finishing operation, and that the significant shift in Pater's attitude towards literary expression occurred between the second and third editions. As previously mentioned, the second text, in all the quotations given, can generally be taken to be identical with that of the first unless specifically noted.

And though the general tendency of the textual variations in the present category is to explain, elucidate, and even omit many foreign words and phrases, I think one can conclude, particularly from the first illustration given above (where a Greek word is introduced into the text for the first time in the third edition), that such a tendency is only another aspect of Pater's first intention throughout the revision of clarifying thought and expression.

F   *Changes affecting sentence structure*

There are, in all, precisely one hundred instances in the revision of *Marius the Epicurean* where sentences as such are altered. Over half of these, however, must be discounted at once as being, in effect, no more than minor punctuation changes — in particular, Pater invariably suppresses from the third edition his grammatical quirk of using a dash in the place of a period stop. And in addition to these, there are a number of other occasions where the change is no more than token, e. g.

1. From that time the distress increased rapidly downwards — *omnia tum vero vitai claustra lababant* — and soon the cold was mounting, with sure pace, from the dead feet to the head.

   I 124 1. 26

3. From that time the distress increased rapidly downwards. *Omnis tum vero vitai claustra lababant;* and soon the cold was mounting with sure pace from the dead feet to the head.   I 125 1. 6

Occasionally the change becomes essential in the course of unwinding and simplifying an unnecessarily tortuous sentence. Here the reason can be said to be mere logical necessity:

1. He was admiring the peculiar decoration of the walls coloured like rich old red leather, (in the midst of one of them was depicted, under a trellis of fruit one might have gathered, the figure of a woman knocking at a door with wonderful reality of perspective,) when the summons came;   I 228 1. 11

3. He was admiring the peculiar decoration of the walls, coloured like rich old red leather. In the midst of one of them was depicted, under a trellis of fruit you might have gathered, the figure of a woman knocking at a door with wonderful reality of perspective. Then the summons came;   I 232 1. 14

And there is one instance where the change seems to be dictated almost entirely for rhythmic reasons. In the following instance it is notable that the revised version is considerably superior in this respect:

1. And at no period of its history had the material Rome itself been better worth seeing; lying there, as complete as that world of pagan intellect which it represented in every phase of darkness and light;

the various work of many ages falling harmoniously together in it, and as yet untouched save by time, adding the final grace of a rich softness to its complex expression.   I 184 1. 17

3. And at no period of history had the material Rome itself been better worth seeing — lying there not less consummate than that world of pagan intellect which it represented in every phase of its darkness and light. The various work of many ages fell here harmoniously together, as yet untouched save by time, adding the final grace of a rich softness to its complex expression.

                                                          I 187 1. 17

There are also a few instances of where Pater has decided that a semi-colon or dash in the first edition has been used to join statements that he now thinks are too far removed from each other to be included in the same period. The following examples show where this tighter and closer conception of the sentence has necessitated some breaking down:

1. Marius gazed after his companion of the day, as he mounted the steps to his lodging, singing to himself, as it seemed — Marius could not distinctly catch the words.   I 199 1. 22

3. Marius gazed after his companion of the day, as he mounted the steps to his lodging, singing to himself, as it seemed. Marius failed precisely to catch the words.   I 202 1. 25

1. The orchard or meadow, through which their path lay, was already grey in the dewy twilight, though the western sky, in which the greater stars were visible, was still afloat with ruddy splendour, seeming to repress by contrast the colouring of all earthly things, yet with the sense of a great richness lingering in their shadows.

                                                          II 118, 1. 14

3. The orchard or meadow, through which their path lay, was already gray with twilight, though the western sky, where the greater stars were visible, was still afloat in crimson splendour. The colour of all earthly things seemed repressed by the contrast, yet with a sense of great richness lingering in their shadows.

                                                          II 113 1. 5

The majority of the examples of interest, however, reveal Pater's increasing use of shorter sentences for climacteric moments. The most obvious of these are when sentences are broken down in order to give a frankly dramatic effect:

1. And after an hour's feverish dreaming he awoke — with a cry, it would seem, for someone had entered the room with a light; but

the footsteps of the youthful figure which approached and sat by his bedside were certainly real.   I 33 1. 12

3. And after an hour's feverish dreaming he awoke — with a cry, it would seem, for some one had entered the room bearing a light. The footsteps of the youthful figure which approached and sat by his bedside were certainly real.   I 33 1. 15

1. There are witches there who can draw down the moon, or at least the lunar *virus* — that white fluid she sheds; to be found, so rarely, "on lofty, heathy places; which is a poison, and a touch of which will drive men mad."   I 62 1. 18

3. Witches are there who can draw down the moon, or at least the lunar *virus* — that white fluid she sheds, to be found, so rarely, "on high, heathy places: which is a poison. A touch of it will drive men mad."   I 62 1. 22

1. In fifty years of peace, broken only by that conflict in the east, from which Lucius Verus had brought back the plague among other curiosities, war had come to seem but a mere romantic, superannuated incident of by-gone history; and now it was almost upon Italian soil.   I 190 1. 19

3. In fifty years of peace, broken only by that conflict in the East from which Lucius Verus among other curiosities brought back the plague, war had come to seem a merely romantic, superannuated incident of bygone history. And now it was almost upon Italian soil.   I 193 1. 17

1. The fairest products of the earth seemed to be dropping to pieces, as if in men's very hands, around him; and still, how real was their sorrow, and his!   II 144 1. 16

3. The fairest products of the earth seemed to be dropping to pieces, as if in men's very hands, around him. How real was their sorrow, and his!   II 140 1. 4

1. In that brief period of peace (the church emerging for a while from her jealously guarded subterranean life) the severity of her earlier rule of exclusion had been somewhat relaxed; and so it came to pass that, on this morning, Marius saw for the first time the wonderful spectacle — wonderful above all in its evidential power — of those who believed.   II 146 1. 16

3. In that brief period of peace during which the church emerged for awhile from her jealously guarded subterranean life, the rigour of an earlier rule of exclusion had been relaxed. And so it came to pass that on this morning Marius saw for the first time the wonder-

ful spectacle — wonderful, especially, in its evidential power over himself, over his own thoughts — of those who believe.

II 141 1. 21

Even more often, Pater makes use of this device whenever he wishes to achieve a greater intensity at a moment of climax in the thought. It will be noticed that most of the following instances are as it were flourishes to conclude an argument or illustrate a statement of belief:

1. As other men concentrate themselves on truths of number, or on business, or it may be on the pleasures of appetite, so, he is wholly bent on living in that full stream of refined sensation; and in the prosecution of this love of beauty, he claims an entire personal liberty of heart and mind — liberty, above all, from conventional answers to first questions. II 32 1. 8

3. As other men are concentrated upon truths of number, for instance, or on business, or it may be on the pleasures of appetite, so he is wholly bent on living in that full stream of refined sensation. And in the prosecution of this love of beauty he claims an entire personal liberty, liberty of heart and mind, liberty, above all, from what may seem conventional answers to first questions.

II 28 1. 2

1. Just then, the merely material world, so often like a heavy wall about him, seemed the unreal thing, and to be breaking away all around; and he felt a quiet hope and joy in the dawning of this doctrine upon him as an actually credible opinion; it was like the dawning of day over a vast prospect with the "new city" in it.

II 80 1. 26

3. The purely material world, that close, impassable, prison-wall, seemed just then the unreal thing, to be actually dissolving away all around him: and he felt a quiet hope, a quiet joy, dawning faintly, in the dawning of this doctrine upon him as a really credible opinion. It was like the break of day over some vast prospect with the "new city," as it were some celestial New Rome, in the midst of it. II 76 1. 21

1. Yes! the reception of theory, of hypothesis, did depend a great deal on temperament; was the equivalent of temperament.

II 103 1. 12

3. Yes! the reception of theory, of hypothesis, of beliefs, did depend a great deal on temperament. They were, so to speak, mere equivalents of temperament. II 97 1. 15

1. What Saint Lewis of France discerned, and found so irresistibly touching, through the dimness of many centuries, as a painful thing

done for love of him by one 'he had never seen, was, to them, a thing of yesterday; and their hearts were whole with it: it had the force, among their interests, of an almost recent event in the career of one whom their fathers' fathers might have known.

II 156 1. 5

3. What Saint Lewis of France discerned, and found so irresistibly touching, across the dimness of many centuries, as a painful thing done for love of him by one he had never seen, was to them almost as a thing of yesterday; and their hearts were whole with it. It had the force among their interests, of an almost recent event in the career of one whom their fathers' fathers might have known.

II 151 1. 13

Against all the above examples, there are two occasions only where Pater has decided that a series of related statements, expressed in single sentences in the first edition, are closely enough related to be joined:

1. And now the nuptial torch gathers dark smoke and ashes; the pleasant sound of the pipe changes into a cry; the marriage hymn concludes in a sorrowful wailing. Below her yellow wedding-veil the bride shook away her tears: insomuch that the whole city was afflicted together at the ill-luck of the stricken house.

I 69 1. 13

3. And now the nuptial torch gathers dark smoke and ashes; the pleasant sound of the pipe is changed into a cry: the marriage hymn concludes in a sorrowful wailing: below her yellow wedding-veil the bride shook away her tears; insomuch that the whole city was afflicted together at the ill-luck of the stricken house.

I 69 1. 17

1. Rhetoric had become almost a function of the state. Philosophy was upon the throne; and had from time to time, by request, delivered an official utterance with well-nigh divine authority.

II 3 1. 16

3. Rhetoric was become almost a function of the state: philosophy was upon the throne; and had from time to time, by request, delivered an official utterance with well-nigh divine authority.

II 3 1. 17

To summarise, all but two of the instances in this category consist of the breaking down of sentences as they stand in the original version. The breaking occurs for a number of minor reasons — to simplify the thought and the punctuation, to achieve a better rhythm; but most significantly, sentences are broken when a dramatic effect is required, either overtly, in descriptive passages, or indirectly, at a climacteric moment in the thought.

G   *Sentences beginning "It was ..."*

The only mannerism singled out for consistently drastic treatment in the revision of *Marius the Epicurean* concerns sentences which begin with the phrase "It was ...". Pater came to regard the phrase as redundant, and there are in all no less than 59 instances of its suppression.

The phrase was avoided in many ways. Sometimes it could be simply deleted:

1. It was on the afternoon of the seventh day that he allowed Marius finally to put the unfinished manuscript aside.
   I 124 1. 20

3. On the afternoon of the seventh day he allowed Marius finally to put aside the unfinished manuscript.
   I 124 1. 26

1. It was to the apparatus of foreign religion, above all,
   I 197 1. 1

3. To the apparatus of foreign religion, above all,
   I 200 1. 2

1. It was to one of those children that Fronto had now brought the birthday gift of the silver trumpet,
   I 242 1. 3

3. To one of those children Fronto had now brought the birthday gift of the silver trumpet,
   I 246 1. 20

1. It was not many months after the date of that epistle that Marius,
   II 217 1. 1

3. Not many months after the date of that epistle Marius,
   II 216 1. 1

Sometimes the whole word order is changed:

1. It was in the vast hall of the Curia Julia that the Senate was assembled to hear the emperor's discourse.
   I 212 1. 3

3. The Senate was assembled to hear the emperor's discourse in the vast hall of the Curia Julia.
   I 215 1. 16

1. It was a very ancient-looking apartment in which Marius found himself,
   I 229 1. 8

3. The apartment in which Marius found himself was of ancient
   aspect,   I 233 1. 12

1. It was therefore a rare thing for him to leave home early in the day.
                                                              II 158 1. 14

3. To leave home early in the day was therefore a rare thing for him.
                                                              II 154 1. 14

But in most instances the sentence is otherwise adjusted:

1. It was twelve o'clock before they left the Forum,
                                                              I 188 1. 25

3. Twelve o'clock was come before they left the Forum,
                                                              I 191 1. 22

1. It was the brow of one who,   I 203 1. 23

3. You saw the brow of one who,   I 206 1. 26

1. It was thus that an obscure synogogue expanded into the catholic
   church.   II 141 1. 4

3. In this way an obscure synogogue was expanded into the catholic
   church.   II 136 1. 9

1. It was a veritable consecration,   II 154 1. 2

3. There was here a veritable consecration,   II 149 1. 7

H   *Revision affecting meaning*

The part of the novel most heavily revised and modified in its thought
is Chapter XVI — "Second Thoughts". This chapter, generally, describes
Marius becoming conscious of the narrow exclusiveness that overcame the
Cyrenaic philosophy — which Pater is using as an equivalent to "aestheticism" — and his realisation that the first Cyrenaics admitted the larger
world of everyday beliefs and superstitions to their view. Marius comes to
feel that the later Cyrenaics, in their rigid exclusion of everything not
immediately perceptible or tangible, lapsed into sterility by cutting themselves off from the richness of accumulated experience informing the trite
and even contemptible trappings of the Greek religion. Marius then con-

cludes that there would be no inconsistency in recognising conventional beliefs once their extrinsic rather than intrinsic value is appreciated.

The argument is intended to be an analogy to the position of his own "aestheticism" in the nominally Christian society of our own day. As much is frankly admitted in the first paragraph:

> That age and our own have much in common — many difficulties and hopes. Let the reader pardon me if here and there I seem to be passing from Marius to his modern representatives — from Rome, to Paris or London.
> First edition, II 15 1. 12

In the course of the chapter, a philosophical history and criticism of the Cyrenaic school is presented, and the ultimate purpose is to justify Marius's eclectic attitude in taking from it aesthetic practice and combining that with the belief in the need for a universal religion and morality. The implication, again, is that Pater's aestheticism need in no way clash with the contemporary "climate", but that it rather performs a marginal though valuable function by invigorating the whole body of belief and practice. In the first edition the analogy is pressed closely and explicitly, and the claims of aestheticism are pitched high. In the revised third edition, however, the more purely philosophical description of Cyrenaicism is deleted and the attempt to give it a respectable position in ancient philosophy abandoned; the analogy with contemporary life is left largely to be inferred; and the more specifically theological aspects of the analogy are entirely omitted. It is open to question whether Pater is himself abandoning his aestheticism, whether, feeling more confident and confirmed, he no longer deems it necessary to plead the cause, or whether the changes were made for external reasons.

Factually, the essential changes are as follows: Pater starts the chapter by saying that Marius was reviewing, at a critical moment in his development, his whole attitude to the world around him, and his 'Cyrenaicism'. Of the latter Pater says, in the first edition:

> What really were its claims as a theory of feeling and practice?
> II 15 1. 17

which in the third edition becomes:

> What really were its claims as a theory of practice, of the sympathies that determine practice?
> II 15 1. 17

The change of "feeling" to "the sympathies that determine practice" may be considered as more philosophically precise, and therefore an attempt at greater definition, but as against this it is notable that throughout the third

edition Pater eliminates wherever possible, when discussing 'Cyrenaicism', all direct reference to emotion and sensation. In the first edition he
goes on to say:

> if it missed something in the commerce of life, which some other theory
> of feeling and practice found itself able to save, if it made a needless
> sacrifice, then, it must be in a manner inconsistent with itself, and lack
> theoretic completeness. Did it make such a sacrifice? What did it lose?
>
> II 15 1. 19

which later became:

> If, therefore, it missed something in the commerce of life, which some
> other theory of practice was able to include, if it made a needless sacri-
> fice, then it must be, in a manner, inconsistent with itself, and lack
> theoretic completeness. Did it make such a sacrifice? What did it lose,
> or cause one to lose?
>
> II 16 1. 2

The word "feeling" has again been deleted, without attempt to compensate.
And the addition of the phrase "or cause one to lose" in the third edition
is a first indication of how much what had been originally abstract argument is now to be put on a personal level.

Pater goes on to say that what he is calling the 'New Cyrenaicism' represents, in one sense, the perennial attitude of youth — "ardent, but narrow in its survey; sincere, but apt to be one-sided, and even fanatical", and
not the threshings and quest for novelty of "jaded men". He continues:

> The Cyrenaic doctrine, then, realised as a motive of earnestness or
> enthusiasm, is not so properly the utterance of the "jaded Epicurean,"
> as of the strong young man in all the freshness of his thought and
> feeling, fascinated by the notion of at least lifting his life to the level
> of some bold, adventurous theory; while, in the first genial heat of
> existence, physical objects, *also* fair and strong, beat potently upon his
> unwearied and widely opened senses.
>
> II 17 1. 21

In the third edition one slight but possibly very significant change is made
— the word "also" (italicised) is omitted. It is difficult to decide whether
it is "some bold, adventurous theory" or "the strong young man in all the
freshness of his thought and feeling" which is put into apposition with
"fair and strong" "physical objects"; the former implies too obviously that
aesthetic theory is itself a product of aesthetic practice, and the latter tends
to confirm the homosexual element latent in aestheticism. What is of interest is not that the word was omitted, but that it should ever have been
used in the first instance.

The 'toning down' of the exposition of aestheticism is soon after carried
further in the alterations to the following passage:

That *Sturm und Drang* of the spirit, as it has been called, those ardent and special apprehensions of half-truths, in the enthusiastic, and as it were prophetic advocacy of which, a devotion to truth, in the case of the young — apprehending but one point at a time in the great circumference — most naturally embodies itself, are levelled down, surely and safely enough, afterwards, as in history so in the individual, by the weakness and mere weariness, as well as by the maturer wisdom, of our nature: — *happily! if the enthusiasm which answered to but one phase of intellectual growth really blends, as it loses its decisiveness, in a larger and commoner morality, with wider though perhaps vaguer hopes.*

II 20 1. 21

In the third edition, the claim of "naturally" is diminished to the observation of "usually", and the whole of the passage italicised, pleading its place in normal development, is omitted.

Saying that "the nobler form of Cyrenaicism" met, at a certain point, "the nobler form of Cynicism", "in a single ideal of temperance and moderation", Pater also claims that this

again was almost identical with the practical wisdom of Socrates, reflecting, in its worthiest form, the conscience of Greece.

II 21 1. 21

— an attempt to place it in an established position in classical philosophy that is entirely omitted in the revision. And after developing the thought that, in the attitude of mind that informs them, many disparate philosophies are in practice much nearer than they at first appear, he says:

Perhaps all theories of morals tend, as they rise to their best, and as conceived by their worthiest disciples, to identification with each other: *the most unlikely neighbours meeting at some point higher than any one of them.*

II 22 1. 11

The generalisation of the passage italicised, which in the context can only be taken as a supreme claim for the 'New Cyrenaicism', is omitted from the third edition; and moreover, the specifically religious associations of "disciples" avoided by the substitution of "representative".

Turning, again, to Cyrenaicism and its place in the classical order, Pater says:

In the gravity of its conception of life, in its pursuit after nothing less than a perfection, in its apprehension of the value of time — the passion and the seriousness which are like a consecration — *la passion et le serieux qui consacrent* — it may be conceived, as regards its main drift, to be not so much opposed to the old morality, as an exaggeration of one special motive in it; it might, with no real misrepresentation, be referred or adjusted to that old morality, as a part to the whole. And if we see this; then comes the question of the value, in all ethical specula- tion, of common terms — of terms, that is, which bring the narrower, or exceptional ideals and tendencies of character, into connection with those which are larger and more generally typical; which, instead of opposing them, explain the former through the latter. Such terms, or conceptions are important in practical ethics, because they largely decide our manner of receiving experience, and the measure we receive of it. They are like instruments, or points of view, which determine how much, and how truly, we shall reflect of life; they lead our atten- tion to this or that element in it, to this or that capacity in ourselves, in preference to another; and, like some optical contrivances in the sen- sible world, they may greatly narrow the field of that experience, in their concentration upon some one, single, though perhaps very impor- tant interest in it, to which they give a false isolation or relief.

II 23 1. 8

In the third edition, only the first five and a half lines of the above passage survive: the larger claim, and then the personal statement of the second sen- tence (in its tone, its oblique reference to something understood but not stated between reader and writer, understood to be *opposed* by the reader) are deleted. Perhaps the obscurest reference of all is to "the narrower, or ex- ceptional ideals and tendencies of character", which, surely, can only mean a self-consciousness on the part of Pater of a specific abnormality. The whole passage, indeed, can be taken as a special pleading in this respect, although it must ultimately remain obscure because Pater does not name, and the context does not provide, what he means by the "common terms" which relate "the exceptional ideals" with "those which are larger and more generally typical".

Pater goes on to say that Marius became aware of the disadvantages of a narrow but intense attitude to life, the attitude which, intellectually, "would take nothing for granted, and assent to no hypothetical or approx- imate truths". He realised that it cut him off from a general sympathy with, and so understanding of, the people around him, who took no such inflexible view. Regretfully, he adds:

If metaphysical acumen had cleared away the metaphysical pretension to know what *is*, that free place might be left for what *appears;* surely, the attractive aspects of morality and religion, as then popularly under- stood, might have ranked as at least φαντασίαι — observable, perhaps amiable, appearances — among the rest.   II 25 1. 5

This sentence, appearing to deprecate the enquiring or 'scientific' spirit of Greek thought, Pater omits from the third edition.

And apostrophising the comprehensiveness of the old Greek religion, "which had grown through and through men's life", and which was, from the aesthetic point of view, "so lovely and so familiar" in its detail, Pater concludes that "a religion like this, one would think, might have had its uses, even for a philosophical sceptic":

> without embarrassing him by any doubtful theory of its intellectual ground-work, or pushing him on to further conclusions, or in any way tarnishing that intellectual integrity, which will not suffer one, out of mere self respect, to pass doubtful intellectual coin.
>
> II 25 1. 24

This passage is omitted from the third edition. The reason is not wholly clear: certainly it is not strictly relevant to the argument, and has that 'pleading' tone which he is so anxious in the revised edition to avoid; but perhaps there is an additional reason for its deletion in that such a criterion as was being advocated in defence of religion was particularly inappropriate in the 1880's and 1890's, when Christianity was still so much under fire from the Rationalists precisely from the point of view of this omitted passage.

Concluding that the Cyrenaic school renounced the Greek religion in their pragmatism, Pater adds:

> and Euemerus, who has given his name to the coldest and thinnest of all phases of rationalism, was one of its accredited masters.
>
> II 26 1. 5

which, as further evidence of his desire not to be too precisely philosophical in the revision, is deleted for the third edition.

And similarly, when Pater immediately afterwards recapitulates that the Greek morality was "a comely thing", "enveloping, so gracefully, the whole of life", the following claim is subsequently omitted:

> The discreet master of Cyrene himself had been in all but entire practical sympathy with it.
>
> II 26 1. 17

The original Cyrenaics, Pater feels, "felt their way ... beyond the narrow limits of clear and absolutely legitimate knowledge; admitting what was not of immediate sensation, and drawing upon that "fantastic" future which might never come" (surely an oblique genuflection to Christianity!). However, the later Cyrenaics would accept nothing but what was immediately known and felt, perceived and apprehended, without a theory to bind it together; and Pater concludes that "the spectacle of their hard, isolated, tenacious hold on their own narrow apprehension, makes one think of a picture with no relief, no soft shadows or breadth of space, or of a drama without repose".

Immediately following this, Pater digresses into a long passage which is the most substantial deletion in the whole revision. It compares the attitude of the Cyrenaics to a 'heresy', and proceeds to describe the place (according to Pater) of heresy in the scheme of theology. It is impossible not to feel, however, that it is an apologia rather than an exposition, and the examples quoted in defence of heresy tend to confirm such a purpose. So that the conclusion, indirectly presented, is that the Cyrenaics had a kind of virtue with them, and that the original Cyrenaics, by the very fact they were capable of giving rise to a 'heresy', have a standing comparable with a theology — the possibility of perversion adding, as it were, to their stature:

Contrasted with the liberality of one like Socrates, their theory of practice, even at its best, has the narrowness — the fanatic narrowness — if, also, the intense force, of a "heresy".

Heresy, theologians are careful to explain, consists not so much in positive error, as in disproportion of truth; in the exaggeration of this or that side or aspect, of the truth, out of the proportion of faith: it being assumed that such exceptional apprehensions of special aspects of the faith, by individual minds, are really provided for in the great system of catholic doctrine. Such a system — such a proportion of faith — is represented for us, in the moral order, by that body of moral ideas common to all Christian lands; which, in those lands, forms a sort of territory common to human society and the Christian church, and which is, in reality, the total product and effect of all the higher moral experience of many generations, and all their aspirations after a more perfect world: it expresses the moral judgment of the honest dead — a body so much more numerous than the living.

And the drift of the evolution of morals has certainly been to allow those theories, which, as I have said, may easily become heresies; theories which have, from time to time, expressed the finer, or the bolder, apprehensions of peculiar spirits — Bentham, Shelley, Carlyle, the old or the new Cyrenaics — theories, the motive of which is to bring special elements, or neglected elements it may be, of our common moral effort, into prominence, by explaining them in unusual terms, or in the terms of some non-moral interest in human life, so much influence, but only so much, as they can exercise, in proportion with that system or organisation of moral ideas, which, in Christian lands, are the common property of human society. And the moral development of the individual may well follow the tendency of that larger current, and permit its flights and heats, its *élans,* as the French say, only so much freedom of play as may be consistent with full sympathy with, and a full practical assent to, the moral preferences of that "great majority," which exercises the authority of humanity; and is actually a vast force all around us. Harmonised, reduced to its true function, in this way, Cyrenaicism, old or new, with its ardent pursuit of beauty, might become, as I said, at the least a very salutary corrective, in a generation which has certainly not over-valued the aesthetic side of its duties, or even of its pleasures. I have been making use of theological terms; and there is another theological term which precisely expresses what I mean. Such or such a heroic quality, say the theologians, is not a precept of the church, but a "counsel of perfection." Such counsels of perfection may become, by exaggeration or wilfulness, heresies; yet they define the special vocations, success in which earns the "special crown," in the case of those for whom they are really meant; and it is in this way that Cyrenaicism, with its worship of beauty — of the body — of physical beauty — might perform its legitimate moral function, as a "counsel of perfection," for the few.   II 28 1. 11

The whole passage is surely the most direct and sustained plea for 'aestheticism' Pater ever made, and certainly the highest claim. It may have been omitted for a number of reasons: by any standards, such direct speech is of course out of place; also, Pater throughout the revision of this chapter has eliminated all that smacks of a personal intervention and philosophical justification. The passage may have given offence by its use of theological terms to approve what Christian theology would no doubt oppose; or it may be that Pater himself began to abandon aestheticism in the seven years between the first appearance and the revision of *Marius the Epicurean.* There is, however, no evidence in his work nor, so far as we know, his life to confirm this last view.

Returning to Marius, Pater says that he was concerned with perfecting "one part of his whole nature — his capacities namely of feeling, of receiving exquisite physical impressions"; and continues:

he hopes, by that "insight" of which the old Cyrenaics made so much, by a highly-trained skill in the apprehension of what the conditions of spiritual success really are, and the special circumstances of the occasion with which he has to deal — the special happinesses of his own nature — to make the most, in no mean or vulgar sense, of the few years of life;   II 31 1. 6

One feels, again, a private allusion in the phrase "the special happinesses of his own nature" because it makes a reference otherwise unsupported in the context, and the mystery is not cleared in the third editon when the word "happinesses" is diminished to "felicities".

Finally, he says Marius will confine himself to "an almost exclusive pre-occupation with the *aspects* of things: their aesthetic character as it is called — their revelation to the eye and the imagination", because such is his natural response to the world around him. But he will also attach himself to "a venerable system of sentiments and ideas, widely extended in time and place", because such a system contains so much of the accumulated experience of the past and cannot help but be an enrichment.

And summarising Marius's position as a Cyrenaic, the following paragraph, related to and concluding the previous long suppressed passage, is entirely omitted from the third edition:

> Cyrenaic or Epicurean doctrine, then — the Cyrenaicism with which Marius had come to Rome, or our own new Cyrenaicism of the nineteenth century — does but need its proper complement. Refer it, as a part to the whole, to that larger, well-adjusted system of the old morality, through which the better portion of mankind strive, in common, towards the realisation of a better world than the present — give it a *modus vivendi*, as the lawyers say, with that common everyday morality, the power of which is continuous in human affairs — excise its antinomian usurpations; and the heresy becomes a counsel of perfection. Our Cyrenaic finds his special apprehension of the fact of life, amid all his own personal colour of mind and temper — finds himself again — though it be but as a single element in an imposing system, a wonderful harmony of principles, exerting a strange power to sustain — to carry him and his effort still onward to perfection, when, through one's inherent human weakness, his own peculiar source of energy fails him, or his own peculiar apprehension becomes obscured for a while.
>
> II 33 1. 10

The chapter ends by claiming that, in associating himself with a larger view of life and yet continuing to strive to perfect his own particular susceptibilities — his pleasure in the visible, his aesthetic response to the things around him — he was fulfilling all the criteria of a "well-considered economy of life".

In the third and fourth parts of *Marius the Epicurean*, Marius comes directly into contact with a primitive Christian community, and there are many passages describing their manner of living, their beliefs (so far as they had settled to an agreed dogma), and the position of the church in those times. In the first edition the 'tone' of these descriptions tends to be at least impartial, if not actually sceptical, and it is notable that in revising the text Pater excises passages plainly critical of Christianity as a religion, passages which imply a 'historical' approach, and even passages which might be taken as derogatory at first sight.

The first of these occurs in the opening paragraph of the following chapter (Chapter XVII), which refers to the barbarian host then gathering in the Balkans:

> The enemy on the Danube was, indeed, but the vanguard of the mighty invading hosts of the fifth century. Illusively repressed just now, those confused movements along the northern boundary of the Empire were destined to unite triumphantly at last, in the barbarism, which, powerless to destroy the Christian church, was yet to suppress for a time the achieved culture of the pagan world: *and with this lamentable result, that* the kingdom of Christ grew up in a somewhat false alienation from the beauty and light of the kingdom of the natural man, developing a partly mistaken tradition concerning it, and an incapacity, as it might almost seem at times, for eventual reconciliation with it.
>
> II 36 1. 1.

In the third edition the text, apart from punctuation changes, remains intact except for the phrase italicised, which is omitted. The phrase gives a value-judgment that is of course out of place in a novel, but it is also directly critical of Christianity.

Parallel with the omission of criticism of Christianity in the revision, there is a hardening of his attitude towards pagan thought and belief. Marcus Aurelius, for instance, is presented on the whole sympathetically in the novel, but when Marius is attempting to sum up the total effect of his philosophy he decides of Aurelius that "his contemplations had made him of a sad heart":

> Resignation, a sombre resignation, a sad heart, patient bearing of the burden of a sad heart — Yes! that was in the situation of an honest thinker upon the world. Only, here there was too much of a tame acquiescence in it.
>
> II 60 1. 1

I think it is significant that in revising this passage Pater changes the neutral "tame acquiescence in it" to the condemnatory "complacent acquiescence in the world as it is".

But immediately following, Pater adds, in contrasting Marius with Aurelius:

> And there was another point of dissidence between Aurelius and his reader — The philosophic Aurelius was a despiser of the body. Since it is "the peculiar privilege of reason to move within herself, and to be proof against corporeal impressions, suffering neither sensation nor passion, both of which are of animal and inferior quality, to break in upon her;" it must follow that the true aim of the spirit will be to treat the body — ωματικός νεκρός — ever a carcase rather than a com-

panion — as a thing really dead, a corpse; and actually to promote its dissolution. And here again, in opposition to an inhumanity like this, presenting itself to that young reader as nothing less than a kind of sin against nature, the person of Cornelius sanctioned or justified the delight Marius had always had in the body; at first, as but one of the consequences of his material or sensualistic philosophy.

II 62 1. 7

In the third edition this becomes:

And there was another point of dissidence between Aurelius and his reader. — The philosophic emperor was a despiser of the body. Since it is "the peculiar privilege of reason to move within herself, and to be proof against corporeal impressions, suffering neither sensation nor passion to break in upon her," it follows that the true interest of the spirit must ever be to treat the body, — Well! as a corpse attached thereto, rather than as a living companion — nay! actually to promote its dissolution. In counterpoise to the inhumanity of this, presenting itself to the young reader as nothing less than a sin against nature, the very person of Cornelius was nothing less than a sanction of that reverent delight Marius had always had in the visible body of man. Such delight indeed had been but a natural consequence of the sensuous or materialistic philosophy of his choice.

II 57 1. 17

By a series of small changes the impact of this passage has been considerably diminished: the qualification "both of which are of animal or inferior quality" applied to "sensation" and "passion" is omitted; the description of the dead body is modified; the phrase "sanctioned and justified the delight" Marius took in the male body glossed down to "sanction of that reverent delight"; and the "material or sensualistic philosophy" of Marius has become "the sensuous or materialistic philosophy of his choice".

The thought is clearly of considerable personal importance to Pater. Contrasting the two versions, the first can be described as almost passionate, with emotion near the surface and some personal article of faith being involved. The purpose of the revision is undoubtedly to put the thought more at a distance, but it still has the marks of an outburst.

Pater describes in Chapter XIX — headed appropriately 'Paratum Cor Meum, Deus!' in the first edition — Marius's gradual awareness of the meaning of Christianity and his recognition that it fulfilled a natural emotional and spiritual need. Pater describes at length how the general concepts of Christianity provided a clear line where his own thought was most confused and incomplete, how it supplied a link with the emotions of the people around him, and how it could at the same time touch him in an intimately personal way. Describing this dawning consciousness abstractly, and as not yet at the stage to lead to conscious acceptance, Pater says:

> How had he longed, sometimes, that there were indeed one to whose memory he could commit his own most fortunate moments, his admiration and love, nay! the very sorrows of which he could not bear quite to lose the sense — one, strong to retain them even should he forget, in whose abler consciousness they might remain present as real things still, over and above that mere quickening of capacity which was all that remained of them in himself! And he had apprehended today, in the special clearness of one privileged hour, that in which the experiences he most valued might as it were take refuge — birds of passage as they were for himself, in and by himself, soon out of sight or with broken wing; yet not really lost, after all, on their way to the enduring light in which the fair hours of life would present themselves as living creatures for ever before the perpetual observer.
>
> II 81 1. 15

This very obscure passage becomes, in the third edition:

> How had he longed sometimes that there were indeed one to whose boundless power of memory he could commit his own most fortunate moments, his admiration, his love, Ay! the very sorrows of which he could not bear quite to lose the sense: — one strong to retain them even though he forgot, in whose more vigorous consciousness they might subsist for ever, beyond that mere quickening of capacity which was all that remained of them in himself! "Oh! that they might live before Thee" — Today at least, in the peculiar clearness of one privileged hour, he seemed to have apprehended that in which the experiences he valued most might find, one by one, an abiding-place.
>
> II 77 1.12

The important change is that what had been described abstractly, as meeting a private need and giving a private satisfaction, is subsequently suppressed in favour of a direct reference to Christianity. It is difficult not to feel that while the first version incorporates some personal allusion, the third version, in the context, strains to convey more conviction than is in fact felt.

Chapter XXII — 'The Minor Peace of the Church' — contains a particularly large number of such changes to a more favourable attitude to Christianity.

Pater is describing the peace and fulfilment Marius found in the household of Cecilia, and the status and achievement of the Christians at that time. One important passage begins:

For what Christianity did centuries later in the way of informing an art, a poesy, of higher and graver beauty, *as some may think,* than even Greek art and poetry at their best, was in truth conformable to the original tendency of its genius: *miscarried, indeed, in the true dark ages through many circumstances, of which the later persecutions it sustained, beginning with that under Aurelius himself, constituted one; the blood of martyrs ceasing at a particular period to be the true "seed of the church."*

II 132 1. 7

The first phrase italicised is changed in the third edition to the more positive "we may think", and the whole of the second part italicised, criticising the Church in the "dark ages", is omitted.

Pater then refers to the flowering of Christianity under the 'Minor Peace' of Antonine, which, he says, is only recovered by "Francis of Assissi" (significantly becoming "Saint Francis" in the third edition) and others with the Renaissance. He concludes:

Constantine's later "Peace," on the other hand, in many ways, does but establish the exclusiveness, the puritanism, the ascetic or monastic gloom of the church in the period between Aurelius and the first Christian emperor, soured a little by oppression and misconstruction, and driven inward upon herself in a world of tasteless controversy: the church then finally comes to terms, and effecting something more than a *modus vivendi* with the world, at a less fortunate moment of the world's development.

II 133 1. 6

In the third edition this passage is diminished to:

The greater "Peace" of Constantine, on the other hand, in many ways does but established the exclusiveness, the puritanism, the ascetic gloom which, in the period between Aurelius and the first Christian emperor, characterised a church under misunderstanding or oppression, driven back, in a world of tasteless controversy, inwards upon herself.

II 128 1. 20

The effect, of course, is to remove the implied stricture upon the Christian Church.

In developing the description of the 'Minor Peace' Pater observes that much of it was due to the "geniality" of the character of Antonius Pius himself. Under his sanction the Church grew and truly came to birth in that for the first time it was able to emerge from secrecy and the catacombs. At this point, in an entirely historical description, Pater quotes Renan:

"The period of the embryogeny of Christianity," says M. Renan, "was then complete. At that date the infant is in possession of all its organs, is detached from its mother, and will live henceforward by its own proper powers of life."

II 134 1. 26

It is difficult to know whether the particular simile gave offence to his contemporaries, or whether Pater later felt that it was in a way blasphemous, that it was omitted from the third edition.

Describing the power of the church even at that early time in checking its more extreme developments, and in creating the beginnings of humanism, Pater says:

And again, it was the church of Rome especially, now becoming every day more and more the capital of the Christian world, *feeling her way already to a universality of guidance in spiritual things equal to that of the earlier Rome in the political order, and part of the secret of which must be a generous tolerance of diversities,* which checked the nascent puritanism of that time, and vindicated for all Christian people a cheerful liberty of heart ...

II 137 1. 19

In this and the following passage, which occurs in the same paragraph, the words in italics are omitted from the third edition:

It was through the bishops of Rome especially, now transforming themselves rapidly in a really catholic sense into universal pastors, that she was defining for herself this humanist path. "*The dignified ecclesiastical hierarchy claimed the right of absolution, and made use of it with an ease which scandalised the puritans.*" And as regards those who had fallen from faith in an hour of weakness, the church of Rome, especially, elected by no means to be as the elder brother of the prodigal son, but rather to pour her oil and wine into the aching wounds.

II 138 1. 12

One can only assume that the motive of these excisions was to remove any suggestion that Pater leant towards the Roman Catholic Church.

In addition to the above, two other chapters, 8 and 14, are notable for alterations affecting meaning.

The death of Flavian is used to mark the division between the first and second parts of *Marius the Epicurean*, and chapter 8, the beginning of Part II, opens with Marius thrown into a condition of despair by the seemingly complete extinction of his friend. One consequence was that he began to concern himself with philosophy, and particularly with speculations concerning the soul. And a further consequence was that his interest in poetry passed to an interest in the literature of thought — that is, to prose. Describing Marius then, Pater says:

> He came of age at this time, though with beardless face, his own master; and at eighteen, an age at which, then as now, many youths of capacity, who fancied themselves poets, secluded themselves from others chiefly in affectation and vague dreaming, he secluded himself indeed from others, but in a severe intellectual meditation, the salt of poetry, without which all the more serious charm is lacking to that imaginative world, *which for him had revealed itself earlier in a spontaneous surrender to the dominion of outward impressions.*
>
> I 136 1. 9

There is no reason in the context of this chapter why the phrase in italics was deleted in the third edition, so that it can only be taken as further evidence of Pater's desire to minimise the sensuous aspect of aestheticism. But as a measure, it is interesting to note that shortly afterwards Pater gives, incidentally, one of the rare physical descriptions of Marius. His companions are wondering at the change in his bearing:

> Was he secretly in love, perhaps, whose toga was so daintily folded, and who was always as fresh as the flowers he wore;
>
> I 137 1. 21

This passage is unaltered in the third edition.

> Marius spent his time reading:
>
> those writers, chiefly, who had made it their business to know what might be thought concerning the strange, enigmatic, personal essence, which had *certainly* seemed to go out altogether, along with the funeral fires.
>
> I 137 1. 26

The word "certainly" is omitted from the third edition. The alteration is slight, but perhaps more important than at first sight. Admittedly it is an intensive word, not necessary to the literal meaning, but its implication in the context is to give the impression that the author is personally committing himself to the fact that there is no existence after death. If this view is valid, then the change must be related to Pater's concern not to give unnecessary offence to Christianity at the time of the revision.

Pater goes on to describe Marius's absorption with Heraclitus; but as with many others, Marius stopped with his initial paradox of the constant flux or change in all things. Marius then inclined to the philosophy of the school of Cyrene, which happily accepted the limitations implied in the Heraclitan paradox and made of it a virtue. Combined with a temperament of moderation, it took as its thesis that all impressions and experiences are limited to moments in time, and the purpose of life was therefore to experience as many of them as possible. Such an attitude, again paradoxically, "became a stimulus towards every kind of activity".

Pater concludes that its special relevance for Marius was that:

> With Marius, then, the influence of the philosopher of pleasure depended on this, that in him a doctrine, originally somewhat acrid, had fallen upon a rich and genial nature, capable of transforming it into a theory of practice which seemed to many to have no inconsiderable stimulative power towards a fair life. What Marius saw in him was the spectacle of one of the happiest temperaments coming, as it were, to an understanding with the most depressing of theories; accepting the results of a metaphysical system to nearly every one so sterile, a system which seemed to concentrate into itself all the weakening trains of thought in earlier Greek speculation, and making the best of it; turning its hard, bare truths, with a wonderful tact, into precepts of a most delicately honourable life.
>
> I 147 1. 15

There are some important alterations to this passage in the third edition. The hesitant qualification "which seemed to many to have no inconsiderable stimulative power" is changed to the assenting "of considerable stimulative power"; the phrase "to nearly every one so sterile" applied to the Cyrenaic system, is omitted; as also is the claim that it created a "delicate wisdom" (!). From these changes there can, I feel, be little doubt that by the time of the later edition Pater was more firmly confident and emphatic in his own aesthetic attitude, though more discreet in his recommendation of it to others. And he goes on to say that Marius accepted the principle of "the subjectivity of knowledge", and claims that certain philosophers have avoided the question, and that mankind at large "dissipate (it) by "common", but unphilosophical, sense, or by religious faith". It is probably important that the latter phrase is not omitted in subsequent editions.

Marius then accepted the Cyrenaic doctrine with a whole heart:

> So the *merely* abstract *sceptical* apprehension that the little point of the present moment alone really is, between a past which has just ceased to be and the future which may never come, became practical with Marius, as the resolution, as far as possible, to exclude regret and desire, and yield himself to the improvement of the present with an absolutely disengaged mind.
>
> I 150 1. 12

This moment of climax in the book remains in the third edition, but intensified by the deletion of "merely" and "sceptical" in the opening phrase.

So Marius, under sanction of the Cyrenaic philosophy, abandoned all further dealings with metaphysics; he realised that "the first practical consequence of the metaphysic which lay behind that perfect manner (i. e. Cyrenaicism), had been a strict limitation, almost the renunciation, of metaphysical enquiry itself".

Summarising the Cyrenaic 'philosophy', Pater says:

> To be absolutely virgin towards a direct and concrete experience, to rid ourselves of those abstractions which are but the ghosts of by-gone impressions — of the notions we have made for ourselves, and which so often do but misrepresent the experience they profess to represent — idola, the idols, or false appearances, as Bacon calls them later — to neutralise the distorting influence of metaphysical theory by an all-accomplished theoretic skill — it is this hard, bold, sober recognition, under a very "dry light," of its own proper aims, in union with a habit of feeling which on the practical side may leave a broad opening to human weakness, that gives to the Cyrenaic doctrine, to reproductions of that doctrine in the time of Marius or in our own, their gravity and importance.
>
> I 152 1. 19

It is perhaps of great importance that this passage remains wholly intact in the third edition, except that the curiously obscure reference to the danger of Cyrenaicism when combined with "a habit of feeling which on the practical side may leave a broad opening to human weakness" is enlarged to "... may perhaps open a wide doorway ..." The reference is certainly not made more clear, but Pater obviously has a very practical matter in mind, and it seems reasonable to suppose from the whole context that he is referring to homosexuality. Shortly afterwards he reinforces the point by stating "Not pleasure, but fulness, completeness of life generally", was the aim of "that pleasant school of healthfully sensuous wisdom".

Chapter 14, the conclusion of the second part of *Marius the Epicurean*, also contains a number of interesting changes of this nature. It is ironically entitled 'Manly Amusement', and after a short passage concerning Cornelius and conveying the stabilising influence that he exerted upon Marius, though for reasons not known to him (Cornelius of course personifying Christianity in the novel), goes on to describe in detail the games held in honour of Lucius Verus and Lucilla and dedicated to Diana. Aurelius is present, and Marius observes him throughout the spectacle; and Marius's consciousness of their differing reactions to the cruelty involved is the means whereby he realises there can be no effective sympathy between them. It was necessary, of course, to show that Marius was exceptional in the Roman world in objecting to the games on what might be called 'humanitarian' grounds alone: the Christians, as Cornelius, showed their disapproval by not attending them (apart from the fact that they were ofen among the victims), but Marius is as yet unaware of Christianity, and the practices at the games were still an accepted feature of Roman life. Thus the description of the games in the amphitheatre has an important place in the structure of the novel, symbolising Marius's departure from the influence of Aurelius, and effectively establishing the sympathy he later achieves for Cornelius and Cecilia, and thus with Christianity.

Any description of the Roman games must inevitably be nauseous to the modern reader on account of their cruelty and sadism. It might be felt that this reaction could be taken for granted without undue detail, and especially here where it can be said to be out of keeping with the tone of the book as a whole. However, what is remarkable in this chapter is not merely the amount of detailed description that is given, but the emotional attitude with which it is presented. The changes that occur in the third edition must ultimately be referred to Pater's subsequent awareness of, and concern to amend, this factor.

Pater's attitude in the first edition is wholly ironical, as for instance:

> the blazing arena, (was) re-covered, at intervals, during the many hours' show with clean sand for absorbing certain great red patches there,
>
> I 252 1. 25

but the later edition tends to substitute explicit indignation and disapproval. Thus, describing the arena before the games begin:

> Along the subterranean ways that led up to it, the sound of an advancing chorus was at last heard, chanting the words of a sacred Song, or Hymn to Diana; for, after all, the spectacle of the amphitheatre was still a religious occasion; its bloodshed having, in a manner, a sacrificial character, tending conveniently to soothe the humane sensibilities of so religious an emperor as Aurelius; who in his fraternal complacency had consented to preside over the shows.
>
> I 254 1. 6

In the third edition, "its bloodshed having, in a manner, a sacrificial character" becomes "To its grim acts of bloodshed a kind of sacrificial character still belonged in the view of certain religious casuists", and the word "religious" applied to Aurelius is discarded as unfit for irony and the more discreet "pious" substituted. The capital letters granted to "Song" and "Hymn" in the first edition are removed, also.

Similarly, when near the end of the chapter Pater describes Aurelius as complacent towards and indifferent to the scene before him, he says by contrast of Marius:

> He at least, the humble follower of the eye, was aware of a crisis in life — in that brief obscure existence — a fierce opposition of real good and real evil, around him; the issues of which he must by no means compromise or confuse; but of the antagonisms of which the wise man was, certainly, unaware. I 259 1. 9

Pater later felt it necessary to leave no possible doubt of the irony intended in the word "wise" applied to Aurelius, and places it in quotation marks. In these and similar ways, throughout the chapter, Pater is concerned to place himself, emotionally, at a greater distance from the scene described.

But there is an ambiguity. Perhaps the most revolting passage in the chapter is the following:

> Scaevola might watch his own hand consuming in the fire, in the person of a criminal, willing to redeem his life by an act so delightful to the eyes, the very ears, of a curious public. If the part of Marsyas was called for, there was a criminal condemned to lose his skin. It might be almost edifying to study minutely the expression of his face, while the assistants corded and pegged him to the bench, cunningly; the servant of the law waiting by, who, after one short cut with his knife, would slip the man's leg from his skin, as neatly as if it were a stocking — a finesse in providing a due amount of suffering for criminals, only brought to its height in Nero's living torches. I 256 1. 20

The only alteration to this passage is an intensification: the opening phrase becomes "Scaevola might watch his own hand consuming, crackling, in the fire".

This change should perhaps be related to what I think is the strangest of all the alterations in the textual history of *Marius the Epicurean*. In Chapter 20, describing the banquet at which Apuleius was present, the following passage occurs in the first edition:

> It was then that the good man's son bethought him of his own favourite animal, which had offended somehow, and been forbidden the banquet — "I mean to shut you in the oven, awhile, little soft, white thing!" he had said, catching sight, as he passed an open doorway, of the great fire in the kitchen, itself festally adorned, where the supper was preparing; and had so, finally, forgotten it. And it was with a really natural laugh, for once, that, on opening the oven, he caught sight of

the animal's grotesque appearance, as it lay there, half-burnt, just within the red-hot iron door. II 99 1. 3

This passage is suppressed from the second and subsequent editions.

The passage is the more remarkable when one remembers that Pater's biographers frequently mention his own fondness for cats. It is, perhaps, the most calmly sadistic passage of imaginative writing one can recall, and related to his delight in the 'Golden Ass' and the description of the Roman games in Chapter 20, must probably be interpreted, psychologically, as revealing an innate element of sadism in Pater's own personality. One final passage may be quoted here as evidence of emotional abnormality; it occurs in Chapter 22, 'The Minor Peace of the Church':

"You would hardly believe," writes Pliny to his wife, "what a longing for you possesses me. II 125 1. 24

In the third edition this becomes:

"You would hardly believe," writes Pliny — to his own wife! — "what a longing for you possesses me. II 121 1. 5

There is no possible explanation of this change in the context; it can therefore only lie in Pater's own emotional condition.

CHAPTER IV

CONCLUSIONS

The essay on "Style" and the revision of *Marius the Epicurean* are the two great interlocking events of Pater's life between the years 1888 and 1892. But "Style" can be said to have begun long before, for Pater had from the first certain leading ideas about literary art that informed his own practice, and the five years devoted to the composition of *Marius* no doubt helped to make those ideas more explicit and self-conscious. After the first publication of *Marius* in 1885 there followed three years of fugitive activity before he prepared, in the middle of 1888, the book-review that led to the essay on "Style". Very probably, however, the essay represents not so much the acquisition of any important new ideas and concepts — that is, there is little perceptible change in his own style before and after — as the crystallising and rationalising of his own habits. But certainly it gave him a more logical and satisfying theory upon which to proceed, and was so important in his own eyes that it demanded the instant revision of *Marius* that has been indicated. Since Pater was 49 when he wrote "Style" and had a considerable body of published work already behind him, it is surprising that an event of such critical importance in his own career should have happened at so late an age. Alternatively, one can feel that the 'introversion', as it were, implied by the essay, the dwelling on first principles and then the time spent revising a published work rather than commencing a new one, stands for a relative failure of his creative impulse, for little of his best work was accomplished after 1888. The balance probably points to the latter. All the evidence, however, confirms more generally the estimate of those critics who have taken the essay as central to any consideration of his work as a whole. It can be treated as the summit of his literary career, though had he lived longer it might have been but a point of transition. At least, in that it caused him to turn back to the already completed *Marius* and further revise it, the essay can be taken as a very well considered statement, representing as totally as possible in such length his beliefs about the practice and the purpose of literary art, even of all art in general.

And if in fact the essay on "Style" does assume so much importance in Pater's work, one must immediately say how disappointing it is as a work of literary criticism. The essay, baldly, is a hotch-potch. It touches on literary practice, a theory of literature, and aspects of aesthetics, all in a relatively short space. But what holds it together and gives it a deceptive sense of completeness is not any consistent logical structure but a unity of *feeling*. This is so strong, and comes from such a forcible sense of conviction, that its entirely logical weaknesses are easily overlooked because they are not, ultimately, relevant. The essay is a work of literary art, not literary criticism, which sets out, in Pater's terms, to persuade rather than to prove. But there is little doubt that Pater intended it as criticism, and that perhaps can be used as justification for treating it as such here. Those aspects bearing directly on the revision of *Marius* will be dealt with first, and then the conclusions that can be drawn from the revision itself, before considering some of the larger and more general points in the essay.

1

For the direct influence of "Style" upon the textual history of *Marius* one can point to a number of general intentions that underlie the changes not concerned with sense. Numerically, the largest group of changes result from a desire to clarify the thought expressed by each sentence as it stands in the first and second editions, or in descriptive passages to give a more concrete image or picture. In such changes it is clear that Pater has himself tried to ascertain his own meaning more exactly, and when he felt he had done so has adjusted the sentence accordingly. Substitutions have been made for the original wording for this purpose, words and phrases have been added or omitted, and even the word order changed: so that the number of sentences in the whole work unaffected at all to this end is a small minority. But so fine is the degree to which Pater insisted on this objective that it is occasionally difficult to feel convinced of the value of some of the changes he made.

A second group of changes results from an attempt to *simplify* the text of the earlier editions. The changes in punctuation are almost all under this heading, and there are many changes of word order and sentence construction that have the same purpose. Similarly, there are a number of verbal changes aimed at intensifying the original text in order to give it at some chosen point a stronger impact. Paradoxically, the few occasions when sentences in the first edition are amalgamated in the third have, in their context, a simplifying purpose.

A further large number of changes is made to achieve a better or more varied rhythm, or greater euphony. Words are again substituted, rearranged, or added for this reason, as well as to avoid assonance and alliteration; there is even an instance of a sentence being recast apparently for rhythmic reasons alone.

The rest of the stylistic changes are concerned with what might be called weaknesses in the original text — the verbal changes of a more mechanical nature. These include the occasions when Pater goes out of his way to vary an obvious or hackneyed expression; to delete neologies, tautologies, and unnecessary particles and qualifications; to change sentence structures in order to eliminate his own grammatical idiosyncracies; and also to avoid pedantic matter, including foreign words and quotations.

Towards the end of the essay on "Style" Pater says:

> Afterthoughts, retouchings, finish, will be of profit only so far as they too really serve to bring out the original, initiative, generative, sense in them. (i. e. words)

and the sentence might stand as the complete expression of his intentions in revising *Marius*. He gave, as the first condition of all good writing, the quality of 'truth' — "the finer accommodation of speech to that vision within" — and this consideration with its attendant concern for clarity and smoothness of expression, lies ultimately behind all the revision of *Marius* other than those chapters altered in meaning. Whatever particular form the revision took, it can be said that the motive at each point was to express, if possible, the meaning more completely and precisely, and that Pater proceeded to test every sentence by this standard. Every phrase and clause was scrutinised to see whether it gave up its meaning clearly, exactly, and euphoniously, and was changed in some way if it could be made to do so in any of these respects. There is no suggestion that any charge of 'obscurity' prompted the revision, because for the most part the greater clarity and precision achieved in the third edition was, by any larger standard, slight. And though Pater often expressed the content of *Marius* more simply in the third edition it was not for any worship of simple words in themselves, but only as a means of presenting the thought more clearly when appropriate. The meaning, in other words, was never sacrificed for verbal simplicity, each shade, nuance, and implication being retained and made more explicit if possible.

The relation, then, between "Style" and the textual history of *Marius* is mostly at the level of Pater's principle of 'truth': the principle from which the essay itself stems, and which became the obsession that drove

Pater to revise *Marius* in its light. Because it is so general, and defies any adequate summary statement, perhaps its force is best illustrated by recalling that it compelled Pater to spend three more years on a work to which he had already devoted nearly five years exclusive attention. In terms of sheer labour, this puts *Marius* above *Madame Bovary*, a fact that probably did not escape him.

2

The aspect of the revision that strikes as most curious is that Pater felt he could dismantle *Marius* into its component sentences, and then revise each as an entity in itself — an undertaking rather like cleaning a watch. For though the essay on "Style" gives little support for such a view, it is clear from the revision that for Pater the art of writing was synonymous with the composition of sentences. The revision shows no departure from his previous habit of treating each sentence as virtually complete in itself, with a carefully and consciously elaborated shape and rhythm. Pater's trade-mark as a writer, of course, consists in his sentences.

The point is so important in considering Pater that it perhaps merits some detailed attention.

The reader of Pater's prose soon becomes aware that a definite pause is essential after each sentence in order to adjust oneself to the rhythm of the next. Each sentence carries a complete impact and impression of its own, so that complementary sentences rarely occur. Such a manner is unusual, and we are so much more used to authors who think in terms of paragraphs and their total impression that Pater's method comes as somewhat of a shock.

Most writers are so obsessed with the concrete meaning and the general impression they wish to convey that individual sentences become only subsidiary means to that end, and thus complementary, antithetical, and elliptical sentences inevitably occur in the course. The reader has from experience become used to reading works as such, hurrying through the paragraph or section and pausing if necessary then, because only then is the impression complete. It is possible to say, generally, that when an author thinks in paragraphs, the sentences, logically, are closely related. The impression of such a paragraph is not just an accretion of the sentences, but something greater than the sum because the relations of the sentences each to each other also add meaning to the whole. Compared with Pater's method, such a way of writing can convey an almost physical sense of movement, because the quality of 'mind', in Pater's sense, goes forward in leaps.

Perhaps the following passage, taken from Chapter II of G. K. Chesterton's *Napoleon of Notting Hill*, will convey what I am wishing to say:

> The reason can be stated in one sentence. The people had absolutely lost faith in revolutions. All revolutions are doctrinal — such as the French one, or the one that introduced Christianity. For it stands to common sense that you cannot upset all existing things, customs, and compromises, unless you believe in something outside them, something positive and divine. Now, England, during this century, lost all belief in this. It believed in a thing called Evolution. And it said, "All theoretic changes have ended in blood and ennui. If we change, we must change slowly and safely, as the animals do. Nature's revolutions are the only successful ones. There has been no conservative reaction in favour of tails.
>
> And some things did change. Things that were not much thought of dropped out of sight. Things that had not often happened did not happen at all. Thus, for instance, the actual physical force ruling the country, the soldiers and police, grew smaller and smaller, and at last vanished almost to a point. The people combined could have swept the few policemen away in ten minutes: they did not, because they did not believe it would do them the least good. They had lost faith in revolutions.

Very few sentences here are balanced and complete in themselves. When read consciously in sentences, the effect is disjointed and the impression blurred. Read more quickly, it is clear that the relation of the sentences is sometimes as important as the sentences themselves; for instance

> The reason can be stated in one sentence. The people had absolutely lost faith in revolutions.

These two sentences are one in meaning; the first is confessedly an introduction to the second, and a writer thinking like Pater in terms of sentences would, if he admitted the first one at all, separate them normally with a colon, never a period stop, for in that way the logical relation would be emphasised and a balance achieved. What is achieved here in addition to meaning, however, is an impact. The first sentence is used solely to underline the second and to give it greater force. The writer's habit of thinking in paragraphs is illustrated, also, by the deliberate evocation of the second sentence in the last one by using almost identical words:

> The people had absolutely lost faith in revolutions.
> They had lost faith in revolutions.

Nothing is added to the sense of the whole, but a 'cemented' effect is achieved, and a sense of movement given by the reference back. But it is exactly the kind of redundant wording that Pater was at pains to eliminate in *Marius* when he revised it.

Whereas the method of Chesterton can be compared to the spokes of a wheel in the way that the sentences are co-ordinate yet converge in the meaning of the paragraph as a whole, the method of Pater, each sentence being rounded off and complete in itself, and linked only by association with its predecessor and successor, can be described as a chain. In illustration, the opening paragraph of *Marius* can be usefully contrasted with the passage above from Chesterton:

> As, in the triumph of Christianity, the old religion lingered latest in the country, and died out at last as but paganism — the religion of the villagers — before the advance of the Christian Church; so, in an earlier century, it was in places remote from town-life that the older and purer forms of paganism itself had survived the longest. While, in Rome, new religions had arisen with bewildering complexity around the dying old one, the earlier and simpler patriarchal religion, "the religion of Numa," as people loved to fancy, lingered on with little change amid the pastoral life, out of the habits and sentiments of which so much of it had grown. Glimpses of such a survival we may catch below the merely artificial attitudes of Latin pastoral poetry; in Tibullus especially, who has preserved for us many poetic details of old Roman religious usage.
>
> > At mihi contingat patrios celebrare Penates,
> > Reddereque antiquo menstrua thura Lari:
>
> — he prays, with unaffected seriousness. Something liturgical, with repetitions of a consecrated form of words, is traceable in one of his elegies, as part of the ritual of a birthday sacrifice. The hearth, from a spark of which, as one form of old legend related, the child Romulus had been miraculously born, was still indeed an altar; and the worthiest sacrifice to the gods the perfect physical sanity of the young men and women, which the scrupulous ways of that religion of the hearth had tended to maintain. A religion of usages and sentiments rather than of facts and beliefs, and attached to very definite things and places — the oak of immemorial age, the rock on the heath fashioned by weather as if by some dim human art, the shadowy grove of ilex, passing into which one exclaimed involuntarily (in consecrated phrase) Deity is in this Place! — Numen inest! — it was in natural harmony with the temper of a quiet people amid the spectacle of rural life; like that simpler faith between man and man, which Tibullus expressly connects with the period when, with an inexpensive worship, the old wooden gods had been still pressed for room in their homely little shrines.
>
> First edition.

A paragraph of seven sentences, this! And the principal difference from Chesterton is again in the matter of sentences — Chesterton's simple,

Pater's elaborate and almost geometrical. The reader's attention is concentrated almost by a grammatical trick — it is unusual for Pater to place
the subject of his sentence at the beginning, without an adjectival or adver-
bial qualification.

In the act of sustaining the parentheses, the mere construction of the
sentence is inevitably borne in on the reader, and with it admiration that
sentences should be capable of so much elaboration and enabled to carry
so much weight of thought. Each qualification and parenthesis pursues an
echo, and achieves it, so that the whole sentence becomes a harmony of
thoughts, a minor fugue, with an entity of its own apart almost from the
text. And because each sentence is, as it were, offered consciously for our
examination and admiration, the impression of a book full of them is a
confused one. One rarely admires a lengthy passage from Pater — small
constellations of sentences are sometimes the most that can live together.
And one can rarely end a chapter and feel that something complete has been
said, for there are few overall effects in Pater's work. Finally, the range of
effects that can be achieved is, compared with those possible from Chesterton's method, restricted.

As a consequence of his manner of writing, the experience of reading
Pater is generally an accumulation of fine impressions, co-ordinate but not
necessarily conclusive. There is, inevitably, a point where the elaboration
of sentences begins in time to detract from the impression of the work
as a whole, where the matter loses its urgency and impact from the subtlety
of its pursuit. Also inherent in the presenting of each sentence as complete
and a work on its own is that, by repetition, it acquires an effect that can
only be called hypnotic. The mechanism is simple. A reader sensitive to
the subtlety of sentence construction will pause with each period, and the
accumulation of similar impressions acts with all the hypnotic power of a
drum. Moreover, Pater's method puts a premium upon sentence rhythm.
Where cadence has been so finely wrought, the ear will insist on hearing
the work, and, as is the way with cadence, slowly and lingeringly. Finally,
Pater's method, at least when judged by the effects it produces, appears to
have more in common with poetry than with prose. Such contortion of
syntax in order to give euphony and cadence are what we expect from
poetry, and Pater's comment in "Style" that Dryden's prose is "vitiated by
many a scanning line", and is thus poetic, has less force now that poetry
has tended to elevate rhythm above metre, so that to us his own prose is
considerably more poetic than Dryden's.

These qualities of euphony, rhythm and cadence, highly as they ranked
in Pater's estimation, get only summary and subordinate treatment in the

6   Pater on Style.

essay on "Style". And it is clear that in revising *Marius*, Pater never deliberately allowed the pursuit of them to over-ride his concern to make each description clearer and each thought more precise. They can in fact be dissociated altogether from the personal crisis represented by "Style", for the small number of emendations made for the second edition of *Marius* seem to have been dictated almost exclusively by rhythm and cadence, and changes of this nature are no doubt as frequent in his other work. Nevertheless, in the total number of changes in the textual history of *Marius* they do bulk largely, and proceeding from them to the essay on "Style" one can only be surprised that the essay does not rate the qualities they represent more highly.

Summarising the revision of *Marius* generally, then, Pater went to enormous lengths in his zeal for the quality of 'truth'. The most searching investigation was made of *Marius* between the second and third editions in an endeavour to express his 'meaning' more exactly and precisely. And as consequently the work was revised on a perhaps unprecedented scale, it is the more surprising that it should have been done so entirely within the original sentence structure. Except in those places where the thought of the original has been changed (every instance of which was probably demanded by considerations external to the work), the revision implies that Pater found no fault with his original conception and intentions. He never finds cause to vary, add to, or omit, to any practical extent, the meaning of the text of the first edition in order to intensify or adjust the impression of the *whole*. Instead, it is the component parts, the individual sentences, that are treated in this way, presumably in the belief that if each item were made more perfect, it would automatically be reflected in the whole. The fact that the revision appears not to have been noticed by his critics is sufficient comment. Most readers will agree that the third edition of *Marius* is superior in every way to the first and second editions, but any suggestion that the improvement is equivalent to three years' labour is absurd. In the final analysis, its importance in Pater's eyes has to be referred to his own personality rather than to any objective literary standards.

The essay and the subsequent revision of *Marius* are not related as cause and effect, but as the two products of a period when Pater suddenly became dissatisfied with his previous work, and felt the need first to express his beliefs in the theoretic form of "Style" and then to redeem his dissatisfaction by revising *Marius*. They join hands in the concern he expressed as 'truth'; but apart from this, the *detail* of "Style" has little direct relation to the revised *Marius*.

3

The evidence, however, is thereby the stronger for treating "Style" as a form of credo, as a considered statement of personal beliefs, especially as many of the ideals he puts forward contrast oddly with his own practice.

The first paradox that might be mentioned is his strange insistence on the quality of 'mind' in literary art, for there is little question that his appreciation of the 'architectural' or intellectual qualities in writing is much greater than his personal achievement of them. His most sympathetic reader will admit that most of his work is, generally, shapeless. In "Style", one can easily perceive that there is at every point a very subtle intelligence at work, engaged on fine distinction, and in following his minute shades of subtlety one is too easily persuaded that a profound logical consistency informs the whole. On examination, the intellectual structure, the theory as such, becomes more and more tenuous and every statement so qualified, that it reaches a point where it can scarcely hold any weight of fact or practical application at all. One feels that his principles should, if they are truly universal, at least be easily comprehensible — yet how relative his idea of 'truth', to take an instance, eventually becomes! While there can be no doubting the intelligence displayed in the essay, the fact probably is that the intelligence is not of the logical kind. It would perhaps be more accurate to call it perception, and to say that the essay is a sequence of related perceptions rather than a coherent theory. It is a paean to literary art, a piece of literature that has literature as its subject, and not to be confused with practical, workaday criticism. So that it is disappointing to look to the essay on "Style" as itself an example of the quality of 'mind' it extols.

Its qualities are probably of a quite different order. As often seems to happen in abstract writing and theorising, it tends to become enamoured of its own phraseology — the individual terms becoming meaningless through excess of meaning — and there comes a moment when the whole discussion takes flight and leaves reality altogether. The concrete thoughts suggested by such abstract reasoning — reasoning, that is, that starts to observe the logic of language rather than of the matter in hand — are often suggestive and useful: but it would be idle to pretend that Pater's quality of 'mind' was in operation.

Perhaps the following paragraph taken from the conclusion of the essay will demonstrate this point:

> I said, thinking of books like Victor Hugo's *Les Miserables*, that prose literature was the characteristic art of the nineteenth century, as others, thinking of its triumphs since the youth of Bach, have assigned that

place to music. Music and prose literature are, in one sense, the opposite terms of art; the art of literature presenting to the imagination, through the intelligence, a range of interests, as free and various as those which music presents to it through sense. And certainly the tendency of what has been here said is to bring literature too under those conditions, by conformity to which music takes rank as the typically perfect art. If music be the ideal of all art whatever, precisely because in music it is impossible to distinguish the form from the substance or matter, the subject from the expression, then, literature, by finding its specific excellence in the absolute correspondence of the term to its import, will be but fulfilling the condition of all artistic quality in things everywhere, of all good art.

This paragraph appears to have a logic that is in fact wholly superficial, i. e. linguistic. We have been prepared for such a high degree of abstraction by the many pages of abstract reasoning that have gone before, where, generally, concept has frequently been brought into relief by the concrete, by examples that is. But the sequence of this paragraph is entirely misleading: in the narrow sense, it is nonsensical. Such phrases as, for instance, "Music and prose literature are, in one sense, the opposite terms of art" have no clear meaning whatever in themselves. We accept them, first, because they are striking, and then because of the promise they contain to prove a fact. But the 'fact' turns out to be the arbitrary statement "the art of literature presenting to the imagination, through the intelligence, a range of interests, as free and various as those which music presents to it through sense". The use of the neutral word "interests" to cover both the various appeals of music and the appeals of literature conceals the quite inadmissible suggestion that music's appeal is necessarily emotional and literature's intellectual. Words are here used to masquerade as reason, not express thoughts. Another specious statement later is "If music be the ideal of all art whatever, precisely because in music it is impossible to distinguish the form from the subject or matter ..." The innocent word "If" manages to establish as an axiom a statement that is put forward entirely without proof; and the claim that "it is impossible to distinguish in music the form from the subject or matter" is not less than absurd, seeing that informed or trained music lovers habitually distinguish between them (between 'theme' and 'form', that is) when they listen, and thereby obtain simultaneously a sensuous and an intellectual pleasure. Such statements, again, tell us more about Pater than about music or art. And it is so manifestly doubtful whether any pleasure obtained from art is wholly emotional or wholly intellectual — doubtful, in other words, whether 'sensuous interests' and 'intellectual interests' have any existence other than as phrases — that we can only wonder at such dubious coinage being offered at this late stage in the essay. But even without calling the ideas themselves into question, one can conclude that there is little 'structure', little quality of 'mind', disposing them.

Such criticism would of course be irrelevant if it did not bear directly upon a point Pater himself made much of. With regard to the paragraph quoted, it is useless to press a literal interpretation upon writing that has risen to this level of abstraction. The intention was perhaps something like this: Pater was wishing to convey an ideal of literature that has many of the associations of the word 'pure', and music, owing to its lack of any verbal meaning, comes the nearest to his ideal of any of the arts. He wished, in other words, the aesthetic response to literature to approximate to that of music. And since the art of music is so entirely non-verbal that useful statements can be made about it in only the most elementary and general terms, and it so has no 'theory' of its own of value, Pater gives it one by suggesting it is analogous with his theory of style in literature, thereby of course also extending the universality of the theory. The possible meanings implied in the above paragraph are so extensive that we can only sit back in admiration at its audacity and scope. Such a height of abstraction and pontifical 'truth' seems to have been reached, and by words as innocent as they are striking, that to ask for a literal meaning seems like a vulgar gesture, or at least a breach of taste. Clearly such paragraphs as this, under the cloak of 'reasoning', have an exclusively aesthetic purpose; if one can be so paradoxical, the intelligence itself is being treated aesthetically. In such practice Pater is a superb artist: but it is a shock to feel that Pater himself believed his thoughts were related logically, from his belief evolving the principle of 'mind'; and perhaps it is best to discount the point entirely. But at least we can say that his remark that "... in literary art, as in all other art, structure is all-important, felt, or painfully missed, everywhere ...", when applied to "Style" itself, which is certainly fine literary art but is also not remarkable for its structure, is profoundly untrue.

4

Pater's suggestion in the essay on "Style" that the literary artist should be deliberate and self-conscious about his vocabulary, that he should "winnow" and "search" for words "with his peculiar sense of the world ever in view", in order to find a vocabulary "faithful to the colouring of his own spirit", suggested to me a certain examination of the use of words in *Marius*. The clear conclusion emerged that Pater himself appears to rely on a basic vocabulary, in this personal sense, of nearly one hundred words, and it is the unusual sentence that does not draw at least once upon this special vocabulary. And if it is true that these particular words were "faithful to the colouring" of his own spirit, they would no doubt be of great value in any study of Pater's personality.

The following, for interest, is a list of the words that stood out as used most frequently in *Marius*, with the number of times they occur in the second volume given for illustration. I have classified them as broadly as possible.

Abstract Nouns		Concrete Nouns		Words associated with religion	
art	–15	body	–27	ceremony	–5
beauty	–35	eye	–18	divine	–24
capacity	–18	flowers	–23	moral	–27
culture	–6	gold	–13	religion	–17
delight	–9	perfumes	–3	religious	–18
enthusiasm	–8			sacred	–15
grace	–14			soul	–57
harmony	–13			spirit	–30
ideal	–26			spiritual	–7
intelligence	–10				
taste	–6				
truth	–38				
vision	–32				

'Precious' adjectives		'Intensive' adjectives		'Odd' adjectives	
aesthetic	–7	absolute	–7	curious	–7
beautiful	–17	ardent	–6	dim	–8
blithe	–4	eager	–3	mysterious	–11
comely	–5	fresh	–13	mystic	–9
dainty	–4	grave	–7	peculiar	–21
delicate	–12	great	–87	quaint	–4
discreet	–6	merely	–27	strange	–24
elegant	–4	pathetic	–8	vague	–2
exquisite	–5	serious	–5	vast	–10
fair	–15	sincere	–5	vivid	–6
fine	– 13	solemn	–8	weird	–2
golden	–20	sombre	–2	wonderful	–18
noble	–7				
perfect	–10	Other words			
pleasant	–13	clear	–17		
precious	–4	dead	–36		
pure	–7	gray	–6		
rare	–7	intellectual	–32		
refined	–6	natural	–25		
rich	–10	true	–39		
select	–4	white	–16		
soft	–4				
sweet	–4				

The words associated with religion can, I think, be largely discounted because they are so close to the subject matter of the book, but the rest of the words may fairly be taken as Pater's 'personal' vocabulary.

Looked at generally, what immediately strikes is the 'ideal' quality of the abstract nouns, and the great preponderance of 'precious' and 'intensive' adjectives. — By 'precious' I mean adjectives that carry a sense of delicacy, gentleness, luxurance, and rarity; and by 'intensive', words that give an impression of more than normal tension, unusualness, and extent.

A list of the words put in the order of frequency is highly interesting: Pater uses, in the second volume of *Marius*, the word 'great' 87 times; 'true' and 'truth' 77; 'soul' 57; 'beauty' and 'beautiful' 52; 'vision' 42; 'mere' and 'merely' 39; 'dead' 36; 'gold' and 'golden' 33; 'spirit' 30; 'body' 27; 'moral' 27; 'ideal' 26; 'natural' 25; 'strange' 24; and 'flowers' 23. In an examination of Pater's life and personality, his obsession with these particular words would be important evidence, but what matters here is that there can be no doubt of his contention, in the essay on "Style", that an author expresses much of his personality in his peculiar choice of words.

Turning to particular words, however, there is an odd contrast between Pater's use of some of these 'personal' words and his insistence on 'truth' — at least in so far as it implies that words should have an *exact* meaning. The most flagrant example is the word 'mystic', and the following is a list of some of the occasions when it is used in *Marius*.

"a kind of mystic hymn"	I 112 1. 8
"the goddess herself . . . in her mystic robe"	I 115 1. 11
"the mystic vessel left the shore"	I 116 1. 4
"a delighted, mystic sense of what passed between them in that fantastic marriage"	I 121 1. 14
"And the mystic burden was relieved"	I 121 1. 15
"an inward, visionary, mystic piety"	I 159 1. 12
"— the pleasure of the ideal present, the mystic now —"	I 166 1. 17
"a philosopher whose mystic speculation"	I 230 1. 10
"this mystic Cornelius"	I 251 1. 17
"mystic companion"	II 59 1. 5
"some mystic attractiveness"	II 125 1. 8
"the mystic tone of this praying"	II 149 1. 11
"a mystic amiability and unction"	II 149 1. 19

I hope enough of the context has been quoted to indicate that no consistent meaning for the word 'mystic' can be deduced from Pater's use of it: it is a word with a certain emotional 'aura' that is preferred, without specific meaning, when the occasion demands. And many of the 'precious' and 'intensive' words mentioned above are also used in a similar loose manner and for the same purpose.

None of these 'personal' words is varied or changed to any appreciable extent in the revision of the text.

5

Many of the principles laid down in "Style", but especially the emphasis placed upon the writer's need for 'scholarship' in language, can be related to the conception of the professional 'man of letters'. Pater was well aware of this phrase and its implications, as he shows in the essay on "Sir Thomas Browne", where Browne's informality and unevenness are contrasted with the work of the professional 'man of letters' of later days.

The exact tracing out of this concept would no doubt throw an interesting sidelight on literature, since it is probably coincident with emerging self-consciousness in writers about their work. Perhaps also the growth of specifically literary criticism, of books about books, was simultaneous. However, throughout the eighteenth century authors can be seen becoming increasingly self-conscious of their trade, if only in that they considered themselves firstly as literary artists and no longer as journalists and pamphleteers; and with this grew the idea of authorship as a 'profession'. All professions labour, as a kind of guild activity, to establish their own code, and so the concept of writing as a 'craft', with of course varying degrees of craftmanship, was an inevitable by-product. And since among professionals the common standard is execution — the matter itself being only a means for the exercise of craft — it is easy to see developing the attitude, accepted without question by Pater and basic to his argument, that the craft of writing, like the craft of music or the craft of woodcarving, is a technique capable of being described in general terms and learnt by the apprentice. The art of writing had become, as it were, almost as important to the writer as the matter to be expressed. If this view is accepted, Pater's plea for scholarship in words is tantamount to asking for finer standards of production, and his essay like a textbook for the ambitious learner.

And so also with what follows: "The literary artist is of necessity a scholar, and in what he proposes to do will have in mind, first of all, the scholar and the scholarly conscience". The appeal follows logically, but it is an appeal that few writers would willingly confine themselves to; manifestly, very few artists, in any sphere, would like to feel that their work was directed, in the first place at least, to what in effect is an audience of other artists and near-artists.

The "influence of a philosophical idea" that Pater roots out in Flaubert is probably much more virulently at work in his own ideas of the 'literary scholar' and the writer's 'scholarship'. To give these ideas meaning, Pater assumes that all words are capable of *exact* meanings: that if they have not an exact meaning already, the writer's business is more to supply them with one. Always there is an assumption that, with enough effort and erudition on the part of the writer, the reader can come to know the sense of what he has written *exactly*. Such constant use in the essay of words of an absolute nature — 'exactly', 'precisely', 'true', 'authority', 'essence', 'one beauty', 'all' — remind one of its philosophical pretension.

Dealing with the 'craft' of writing and its 'craftsmanship', it is perhaps not too much to claim that these ideas are largely imaginary — they exist, that is, as the result of a false analogy. But having invented the subject, 'professional' writers were naturally obliged to give the rules of the game. One of the consequent platitudes that has gained acceptance is the notion that words, in the course of time, become 'debased'. What this more accurately means is that the connotation of a word has changed, or that it has been given a subsidiary meaning: but if there is any tendency at all in this matter, the evidence is surely that, rather than becoming more general, words, with the passage of time, tend to become more precise. Constant shiftings and narrowings of meaning make the literary 'craftsman's' work more difficult, reminding him that his material is more like sand than stone; and since it is in the nature of 'craft' to be intensely conservative, it is not surprising to find that the tone of Pater's remarks in this connection is more that of the guardian of the holy temple than the adventurer (if one can convey the idea by metaphor). Since the activity of the artist and the activity of the craftsman are nowadays for the most part clearly differentiated, it is difficult to feel that Pater's observations and principles have any vital relation to literary art.

6

Not unrelated to the previous section is Pater's statement that for "all disinterested lovers of books", a perfect work of literary art will have "something of the uses of a religious retreat". In case this should be taken as another way of expressing 'catharsis', Pater goes on to say that literature, to such readers, will be "a sort of cloistral refuge, from a certain vulgarity in the actual world", in order to emphasise that his meaning is quite otherwise than Aristotelian. From the latter phrase we can assume that for Pater the essential contrast was between the perfection and completeness to be found in certain works of art, and the incompleteness and dissatisfaction of everyday living.

A proper discussion on Pater's attitude to art, especially as detailed in "Style", would beg an aesthetic; and it is important because it is so much the aspect of his work that was taken up in his own lifetime, and has been heavily criticised on many hands ever since (Edward Thomas, in his biography, is constantly chafing at this point). It is the greatest barrier to the modern reader in understanding "Style", at least. But perhaps one can say, by way of general summary, that whereas before Pater the theories of art (e. g. catharsis) had treated art as a means to an end, the aesthetic emotion completing itself in a fresher and purer (or nobler, or more moral, etc.) reception of everyday experience, Pater is the first writer of influence to suggest that the aesthetic emotion could be an end in itself. The theorists of art seem always to have been concerned to fit it in its place, to harness it to a practical end, and to make it subordinate to larger purposes: the novelty of Pater was to dare to reverse this trend. And such phrases as "a certain vulgarity in the actual world", and the concept of art as a kind of "religious retreat", leave no doubt that in his mind not only has the aesthetic emotion a right to exist on its own, but in fact is superior to any other consideration. If art is indeed to be placed at the head of the natural hierarchy, it can of course exist only for its own sake; and the implied derogation of other qualities and activities naturally enraged the moralists.

We know, from the alterations to the "Conclusion" of The Renaissance, and probably also from the alterations to the sence of Marius, that Pater came to fear the consequences of his own doctrines. Pater's intelligence would from the first have held his beliefs in check had he really considered all their implications, and from the fact that it did not one can assume that his beliefs, particularly about the function of literary and other art, are to be referred in the first place to his own personality.

Concerning the nature of his personality it is enough here to mention the essentially *passive* quality of his theory art, its almost feminine nature. The following quotation from "Style" will perhaps illustrate this point:

> "... the literary artist, I suppose, goes on considerately, ... retracing the negligences of his first sketch, repeating his steps only so that he may give the reader a sense of secure and restful progress, readjusting mere assonances even, that they may soothe the reader ..."

What are first remarkable here are the adjectives describing the work's progress — "secure and restful"; allowing for Pater's desire to choose the unusual word, the latter is surely extraordinary. And similar is the use of the word "soothe" towards the end. Behind both words is what Pater assumed his ideal reader expected from literary art, itself no doubt a rationalisation of his own pleasure.

If the aesthetic emotion is to be enjoyed as an end in itself, it goes without saying that it must be highly self-conscious. And since the self-conscious approach to a work of art is usually known by the special name of 'appreciation' (and the volume in which "Style" was published is called specifically *Appreciations*), it would not be unfair to say that Pater's attitude to literary art was almost exclusively at this level. His native sensibility appears to have been so completely saddled and bridled by self-consciousness that he was unable to go beyond a work of art at all — to suffer, in other terms, catharsis — and so the impetus turned back on itself, and examined both itself and the process that brought it into being. Such a motion would explain his obsession with method, and would justify his attention to, for instance, sentence structure, in the intricacy and subtlety of which he has no superior. Its weakness, of course, is that the consequent obtrusiveness of his method leaves the reader room for little more than appreciation also.

7

I should like, finally, to pay a little attention to Pater's concept of (and use of the word) 'truth' — the quality, he claims, that lies behind all good writing. I have so far accepted it without question because I have been concerned mainly to argue from the essay's own premises. It is, however, a critical commonplace now to look askance at abstract words, particularly when they are used in an argument as supporting columns, and I suggest this word will tolerate a little examination.

Nowhere in the essay on "Style" does Pater admit any other situation than the literary artist saying, or wishing to say, exactly what he means in a direct and straightforward manner:

> "The first condition ... must be, of course, to know yourself, to have ascertained your own sense exactly. Then, if we suppose an artist, he says to the reader, — I want you to see exactly what I see."
> "Say what you have to say, what you have a will to say, in the simplest, the most direct and exact manner possible, with no surplusage: — ..."
> "The term is right, and has its essential beauty, when it becomes, in a manner, what it signifies, as with the names of simple sensations. To

give the phrase, the sentence, the structural member, the entire composition, song, or essay, a similar unity with its subject and with itself: — style is in the right way when it tends towards that."

"... in proportion as the writer's aim, consciously or unconsciously, comes to be the transcribing, not of the world, not of mere fact, but of his sense of it, he becomes an artist, his work fine art; and good art (as I hope ultimately to show) in proportion to the truth of his presentment of that sense ... Truth! there can be no merit, no craft at all, without that. And further, all beauty is in the long run only *fineness* of truth, ..."

My point is that from these categorical statements there would seem to be no place in Pater's scheme for writing that is deliberately ambiguous, for allegory, irony, or satire, for instance. Indeed, in that there the author knowingly chooses to say something other than what he means, such writing appears to contradict the principle of 'truth', for the words certainly do not correspond, at least in the literal sense, with the author's intention. The omission is strange, unless Pater meant to imply that such writing is not to be considered as fine art and so able to acquire 'style'. It is more likely, however, that the omission was unconscious because it was foreign to his own taste and inclination.

It is of course possible to say that in the case of allegory the author has indeed a strong and clear vision of what he wishes to say, and that it is this which guides him in his choice of a story, and the form and words in which to set the story. But something is lost in making so neat a statement: taking "The Faerie Queene" and "The Hind and the Panther" as handy examples, it is clear that the superficial story, the vehicle of the allegory, is yet more or less complete in itself and can, if one wishes, be accepted on that level alone. The allegory merely peeps through: it is not explicit at every point. If there were a direct and continuous relation between story and allegory, the principle of 'truth' would apply in a sense, but the relation is rarely a simple *mutatis mutandis*. The fact is rather that the literary artist has two meanings, on different levels, related to but not dependent on each other, and one's pleasure in the reading derives at least in part from the inter-relation of the double theme. Pater's 'truth', if it is to maintain its dignity, must admit to being two-faced here.

Or, thinking of satire, one realises that very few English writers have achieved so limpid, forceful, and effective a literary style as Dean Swift, and that, taken as story, *Gulliver's Travels* might be a model of the exact marriage of thought and word that Pater recommends. It is only too obvious, however, that the immediate story was the least part of the 'intention', perfectly (as the anecdote of the bishop shows) as he succeed-ed in this respect; for it is quite clear that the story conceals some other purpose, a purpose that lends the story its strength and tension, although one would be hardly put to define that purpose closely. It came from a way of feeling, a powerful emotional drive and obsession, and there is no reason to believe that it was any 'clearer' to Swift when he wrote it than it is to the reader today.

The case of irony is interesting. I take irony to differ from satire main-ly in that its wider purpose is not simply to make fun, and in that its reference (or meaning) is usually less clear-cut; nor has it the moral edge of satire. I venture a guess that the presence or absence of a 'second meaning' is the most important item in the value of a work of literary art, and novels in particular seem to retain interest in proportion to the extent they are 'ironical' in this sense. Examples are obvious; but perhaps it is enough for the immediate purpose to mention the irony at the heart of *Marius* itself, as Pater makes plain at the beginning of Chapter XVI. Pater also uses irony in the narrow sense in the description of Aurelius at the Roman Games that has been instanced (p. 77).

And at risk of burdening the point, nonsense and fantasy might be mentioned as bearing no very obvious relation to the concept of 'truth'. Such types of writing may not be placed highly in the aesthetic scale, but the business of classifying has no necessary connection with art, and to deny them the claim of ever being art at all raises the larger question.

Enough, I hope, has been said to show that Pater's concept assumes a highly self-conscious intention to be present always in the mind of the literary artist; and that in some of the works we commonly value the relation between intention and expression is by no means clear and pre-cise — sometimes, indeed, any intention at all is hard to detect.

It is legitimate to point out the exclusiveness of Pater's theory without suggesting that there are ways in which it could be made more embracing. I do not think that the defects are in Pater's theory so much as that any theory must, of its nature, be defective to some extent. Theories of art are apt to be like theories of society or economics — perfect in direct proport-ion to the number of facts they exclude. In Pater's case, his theory at least has the virtue of accounting for the kind of writing he himself appreciated and setting forth the ideals he himself followed, and its value I suggest is principally to this end.

If, however, we dissociate for a moment the concept of 'truth' from its name, I think it is fair to say that the concept might as justly have been called 'identity' or 'accuracy'. An interesting experiment is to substitute, say, the word 'accuracy' for the word 'truth' wherever it occurs in the essay on "Style". I do not think anything appreciable is lost in literal meaning by such a change; what, though, immediately makes itself felt is a considerable loss of impact and conviction. The 'tone' suffers greatly, losing a certain, indefinable oracular quality. Clearly this missing force comes from the aura that surrounds the word 'truth', itself the residue of all the associations that have become attached to it from our past reading and personal experience.

Let us put it this way: there is the word 'accurate', a colourless one usually employed in a factual, scientific context, and there is the word 'true', which means the same thing but carries with it the implication that the thing stated is important or significant. But 'importance' and 'significance' imply relation, not absolute position. The word 'true', most of all, affirms an identity of conviction or feeling between two parties, and it is precisely because one does not feel that identity with Pater that the word stands out like a stump.

'Truth' presupposes an absolute quality, as do many of the abstract words used by Pater in the essay on "Style", and of course the very making of such a theory implies also a belief in statements of absolute value being possible. Scientific theories, it must be noted, are not strictly in this case: they are generally constructions put forward with an emphasis on their provisional character and as a kind of summary of existing knowledge. Theories of art, however, tend to borrow the claims of philosophy and religion, and arrogate the belief in the absolute that they have fostered. I therefore suggest that, on a purely logical level, Pater's use of the word 'truth' amounts to the borrowing of what is, ultimately, an emotional attitude, and could with justice be placed in his class of removable ornament.

The word 'beauty' has a similarly uncomfortable role in the essay. It is used in two senses: first, it is equated with 'truth' ("all beauty is in the long run only *fineness* of truth"), but later on, dealing with ornament, Pater uses the word in the visual sense of particular beautiful things ("the flowers in the garden"). There is an innate conflict between these two meanings, unless the word, like 'truth', is to be Janus-headed. For in the latter sense, beauty is assumed to be inherent in certain things, a part almost of their physical make-up and with no further explanation of their quality necessary; in the former sense, it is a by-product of another quality.

Without pressing 'beauty' further, I want to suggest that this word and the word 'truth' have a function in Pater's essay which is not, to put it narrowly, logical and reasonable. They have no very exact meaning, but they are used as freely as though they had. There is no doubt that Pater went to considerable lengths to ensure as precise a meaning as possible throughout the essay on "Style" also, but certain key-words such as these two have in fact no precise reference though they are fundamental to his argument. They have, it seems, more (for want of a better word) emotional than factual meaning, and their function seems to be to call forth a reaction, like a handshake between friends, rather than to convince. It is taken for granted, in other words, that we are at one with Pater in the value to be placed on these words, and that it is unnecessary to pursue them further. They are responsible, consequently, for the 'tone' of the essay, but unfortunately despite the short time since the appearence of the essay they are the very words we are least likely to feel sympathy with in his usage. I do not mean to assert that the words are inadequate or that we have moved towards preciser definition in this matter: merely that they are words that are going out of use and which tend to cause a vague embarrassment when used now. Perhaps a little speculation on the reason for this will be permitted.

Pater suggests at the beginning of the essay on "Style" that one of the reasons for the predominance of prose in the nineteenth century was the pervading interest in natural science and its concomitant, a relatively humble approach to facts and a valuing of facts for their own sake. What Pater described as a tendency in the 1880's has since become the commonest attitude. And the paradoxical effect of acquiring more factual knowledge is a parallel awareness of the limits of such knowledge, the greater mass of factual knowledge now available revealing more and more the inadequacy of our language to describe and record it (vide almost any scientific textbook). So that it is, I think, a natural reaction for there to be less and less tendency to juggle with abstract words and theories about the unknown (and perhaps unknowable), and little sympathy when the attempt is made. The very act of dealing with absolutes seems to have something illegitimate about it: as though the author were thereby getting a vicarious sense of power over the unknown — playing with words and invoking powers like a medicine-man or a priest.

Such points as I have mentioned are, I believe, among the factors that make it difficult to approach Pater generally, and, more important, to deal satisfactorily with the essay on "Style". Which is a pity, for my abiding impression is of much that is of value in the essay, and in almost all Pater's other work also. I feel very strongly that too much attention has been paid to the least attractive part of his writing, the florid passages that occur from time to time in the early work, and too little to the very fine writing that characterises his later work. Pater is rarely remarkable for what he actually says: to try a judgment, he had perhaps least to say of any major nineteenth century writer. What he did have to say, however, he said with grace and brilliance, and there is an intense pleasure in observing the sheer intelligence that informed it, such as I have tried to give an indication of here.